The
Getaway
Guide I

Second Edition, Revised & Enlarged

The Getaway Guide I

Short Vacations in the Pacific Northwest

by Marni and Jake Rankin

Pacific Search Press

Pacific Search Press, 222 Dexter Avenue North,
    Seattle, Washington 98109
© 1982 by Marni and Jake Rankin. All rights reserved
Printed in the United States of America

First edition published in 1979
Second printing 1980
Third printing 1980
Fourth printing 1981

Designed by Judy Petry

Cover: Mount Washington from Black Butte Ranch

Library of Congress Cataloging in Publication Data

Rankin, Marni.
    The getaway guide I.

    Rev. ed. of: The getaway guide. ©1979.
    1. Hotels, taverns, etc.—Northwest, Pacific—Directories. 2. Resorts—Northwest,
Pacific—Directories. 3. Northwest, Pacific—Description and travel—1951-1980—
Guide-books. I. Rankin, Jake. II. Title. III. Title: Short vacations in the Pacific
Northwest.
TX907.R32   1982   917.95 '0443   82-18784
ISBN 0-914718-76-2   (pbk.)

Wherever you go and whatever you do in the outdoors, move at Nature's pace, seeking not to impose yourself but to lose yourself. If you must leave footprints, make them not with blindness but with care and awareness of the delicate balance around you. And if you must take souvenirs, take them not in your pockets but in your mind and spirit. In preservation lies the promise of renewal.

—Pacific Search Press

Contents

Preface 9

Why Getaways? 11

North Getaways 14
    Rosario Resort 15
    The Islander Lopez Resort 22
    Sudden Valley 27
    Smuggler's Villa 33
    Harrison Hot Springs 40
    The Westin Bayshore 46
    Island Hall Hotel 53
    The Empress Hotel 58
    Laurel Point Inn 66

Central Getaways 72
    La Conner Country Inn 73
    The Captain Whidbey Inn 78
    The Admiralty Resort at Port Ludlow 84
    Ocean Crest Resort 91
    Alderbrook Inn 97
    Lake Quinault Lodge 103
    The Grey Gull 108
    Iron Springs Ocean Beach Resort 115

East-Central Getaways 120
    Sun Mountain 121
    Cannon's Resort 128

South Getaways 137
    Kah-Nee-Ta Vacation Resort 138
    The Inn of the Seventh Mountain 145
    Black Butte Ranch 151
    Sunriver Lodge 159
    Gearhart-By-The-Sea 166
    Tolovana Inn 172
    Columbia Gorge Hotel 178
    Neskowin Lodge 186
    Surftides Beach Resort 192
    Salishan 197
    The Embarcadero 203
    The Inn at Otter Crest 210
    The Village Green 215

Checklist 221

Preface

When we sat down to write the first *Getaway Guide* in early 1979, our aim was to create a ready reference to all the better places in the Northwest available for getaway vacations, preferably on short notice. We had just three criteria: to find places that were comfortable and fun, to provide the complete information needed to make choices between these resorts, and finally to make the book interesting reading.

To our satisfaction, the idea has been readily accepted and people have bought the book and used it as a handy reference from the start, so that our publisher has had to go to reprint a number of times to keep up with the demand.

Meanwhile, we have kept up with the getaways themselves and learned again how pervasive is change, and nowhere more so than in the resort business. Key personnel come and go, facilities are added and deleted, prices go up, seasons are altered, and sometimes whole operations go out of business, while new ones are built and defunct ones remodeled and reopened. We realized we were going to have to revise and update this book periodically if it was going to continue to serve its function of providing useful information.

So here is the result. Every chapter has been changed, some quite extensively, and three chapters have been deleted entirely because the resorts are no longer viable; but six newly discovered ones have been added to take their places.

Many of the changes were brought to our attention by feedback from readers who wrote to us about what they liked and didn't like concerning our subjects. Their advice, moreover, has been an enlightening clue to what people want to know, and it has helped tremendously to make this updated book useful and timely.

We enjoyed doing the original *Getaway Guide*, and, when possible, enjoyed revisiting the places and rewriting the chapters about them even more. We hope the reader will share at least a small part of the same pleasure from his perusal of this material, and then from visiting the resorts—as many as possible!

Why Getaways?

The best vacation is not always an annual two weeks at the beach. Two weeks are fine, but then you must wait eleven and a half long months for the next vacation. Instead, a number of two- or three-day getaways throughout the year take no more total time from work, yet add up to a great deal more fun and experiences than any single vacation could possibly provide.

The secret of the short vacation—the reason it is so satisfying—is that the first few days of a change in scenery and routine are invariably the most relaxing and stimulating. A sudden plunge into a new environment occupies the whole mind. New sights and sounds, especially when they are wholly agreeable, replace the baggage of ordinary cares. It is this initial period of rest and mind clearing that refreshes and rejuvenates, making just a day or two at a pleasant inn seem like a week. We have learned to capitalize on the magnification of those first few days by experiencing them often during the year.

That is the getaway vacation: a trip that takes a minimum of time but offers a maximum of enjoyment and relaxation. You return to the workaday world with new enthusiasm and zest.

Getaways can be long weekends or a few days snatched from midweek. They are always more fun on the spur of the moment. You are tired, overworked, and need a change—suddenly, a chance presents itself to chuck it all for a day or two. Take it! Call ahead for a reservation at a destination that has charm, comfortable rooms, interesting food, access to the outdoors, and stimulating natural surroundings, but is not so far away that the drive would be a chore. Then just throw a few things into the car and go.

This book arose from our realization that we sometimes put off taking little trips simply because deciding where to go and organizing and packing seemed a nuisance. Since we tended to forget which places were most fun or what season was best or what to take, the answer for us was to start a file on good destinations, with notations about what each had uniquely to offer, the distances, and the costs. We also worked up a handy checklist of house arrangements and of items to take with us. All this worked beyond our expectations! It became easy to pack up and go, and we no longer spent the first hour of the trip worrying about what we had forgotten. In time, these notes and lists just naturally expanded into a book so we could pass along the information.

The way to use this guide is to thumb through the chapters until a place strikes your fancy in accordance with the season. Then phone ahead to make sure rooms are available (telephone numbers and addresses are listed) for whatever time you are planning your getaway. Keep in mind that many of the inns have package plans and seasonal rates that will save you money. These change from time to time, so make a habit of asking the reservations clerk what is currently available. Also, except when specifically mentioned, "No pets allowed" is the standard rule.

In estimating traveling time, we have assumed that a trip will have no hitches and that you will drive the legal speed. (If you prefer distances in metrics or just want to get in the habit of thinking in kilometers instead of miles, simply multiply the distances by 1.6.) Do remember that traffic can be heavy, especially in the summer and on weekends, and that any trip involving a ferry ride could be prolonged by waiting in a line at the dock.

At the end of the book, you will find a general checklist of things to do and of items to pack before you take a getaway trip. Special articles that might be needed for particular destinations are mentioned in the appropriate chapters. We like leisurely mornings, so our own trip kit includes a small percolator, a jar of freshly ground coffee, two cups, and a supply of cinnamon rolls. That takes care of breakfast, and we do not have to dress until we are ready to go out for the day. Sometimes, too, we like to take along a continental lunch: French bread, cheese, dry salami, and a bottle of wine. With that tucked into a picnic basket or rucksack, we are set for the day should the impulse strike to take off for parts unknown. If not, these things all keep well and we can use them later.

Dinners are a different story. We like to linger over a fine meal in a pleasant atmosphere, and dinner is the high point of our day. Each trip has been carefully researched to find the best places to eat—either at the inn or in the vicinity—where service is good, food is top quality, and prices are reasonable.

To be included in our book, places also had to have clean, comfortable, modern accommodations, friendly and helpful staffs, and refreshing surroundings with plenty of interesting things to do. They also needed to be relatively close to one of three major cities—Portland, Seattle, or Vancouver, British Columbia.

In order to provide a frame of reference for assessing the cost of a getaway trip we have given on-season rates for rooms for two people. We know, of course, in times when prices of everything are changing rapidly, that this can be a dangerous practice. Nevertheless, if within a few years the prices are no longer exact, at least they will be relative, and you still will be able to compare the expense of one getaway possibility with another.

Many people have asked us, since we have been working on this book, which places we like best and why we have not made comparative ratings of our choices. The answer is that we thoroughly enjoyed every one. If we visited a place we did not want to go back to, we did not include it. The important point is that every one of these places is different. We might like to revisit one today but quite a different one tomorrow, depending on our mood, what we feel like doing and seeing, and how much time is available. Selecting the right place at the right time is what counts. That is why this book is arranged like a catalog; you can compare possibilities and then choose the most suitable.

We hope you will enjoy all of these getaways as much as we have. If you have strong feelings about any place we have mentioned, we hope you will drop us a line. Your comments will be grist for our mill when it comes time to update the book.

North
Getaways

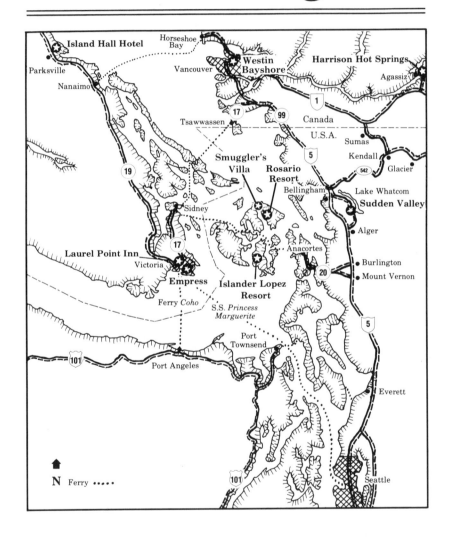

Island Hall Hotel
Parksville
Nanaimo
Horseshoe Bay
Vancouver
Westin Bayshore
Harrison Hot Springs
Agassiz
17
99
Canada
U.S.A.
Sumas
Tsawwassen
1
5
Kendall
542
Glacier
Smuggler's Villa
Rosario Resort
Bellingham
Lake Whatcom
Sudden Valley
19
Sidney
Alger
Laurel Point Inn
Victoria
17
Anacortes
Burlington
Mount Vernon
Empress
Islander Lopez Resort
20
Ferry Coho
S.S. Princess Marguerite
5
Port Townsend
101
Port Angeles
Everett
N Ferry •••••
101
Seattle

Rosario Resort

Distances:

From Seattle—76 miles to Anacortes, 1¼-hour ferry ride, 14 miles on Orcas Island; allow 3½ hours. Via San Juan Airlines, flight time 1 hour

From Portland—270 miles to Anacortes, plus ferry; allow 7 hours

From Vancouver, B.C.—108 miles to Anacortes, plus ferry; allow 4 hours

Features:

Orcas Island known as the "Jewel of the San Juans"; slow paced, friendly, picturesque; has most sun and dry weather in Western Washington; natural characteristics unspoiled; complete resort facilities

Activities:

Hiking, fishing, tennis, golf, swimming, watching wildlife, browsing through shops and craft studios in Eastsound

Seasons:

Year-round; reservations well in advance recommended during summer and for all holidays and weekends

Rates:

$45 to $69 for two people

Address:

Eastsound, Washington 98245, U.S.A.

Phone:

(206) 376-2222; toll free in Washington, 1-800-562-8820

Old Moran mansion now Rosario Lodge

It perhaps comes as a surprise that the beautiful, almost countless islands making up the San Juan archipelago contain only a few really fine year-round vacation resorts. Of these, the oldest and largest is Rosario on Orcas Island. Actually the old Moran estate, it is located on Cascade Bay on the eastern shore of East Sound, the long, narrow, placid neck of water that almost cuts Orcas Island in half.

Robert Moran was mayor of Seattle and a turn-of-the-century ship builder whose yards, among other projects, turned out the powerful battleship *Nebraska* for the United States Navy. His estate on Orcas originally encompassed over five thousand acres, most of which he donated to the state for what is now Moran State Park. The remaining one thousand acres, including his stately old mansion, which serves as the main lodge, constitute the present-day resort.

Recent owners have added a complex of new facilities for the convenience of guests. To their credit, they have kept them well scattered and sited to take advantage of commanding water views, at the same time preserving the sylvan nature and low-keyed pace characteristic of Orcas.

The tempo of the island is immediately evident to every first-time visitor. Its communities are small and picturesque. The natives go out of their way to be friendly, but they are nevertheless proudly self-reliant and determined to live in their own style.

The roads follow property lines and thus make many abrupt right-angle turns, which discourage speed. But that is fine with the islanders, who have always stoutly rejected federal aid for straightening roads because they like the meandering quality exactly as it is.

Around the Rosario Resort it is a common occurrence to see deer browsing amongst the buildings and rabbits on the lawns. This makes for a nature photographer's paradise as well as illustrating the true environmental quality of the island.

Fall is often the most beautiful and enjoyable time of year to visit the San Juans. There are still plenty of warm, sunny afternoons, and the often foggy mornings provide time to read and rest. The leaves are turning color, the air is crisp, and the crowds have all departed, so hikes in the woods and up Mount Constitution are solitary and unspoiled. It is easy to get on the golf course or tennis courts during this season, and the heated outdoor swimming pool is still in operation and refreshing after a day's outing.

Routes and Distances

From Seattle and Portland take Interstate 5 to Mount Vernon and then head west on Washington 536 for six miles until it merges with Washington 20. Take 20 to Anacortes and follow the signs for four more miles to the ferry. Crowds at the ferry terminal vary, but to ensure yourself of having a place on the boat, get to the ferry landing a half hour before sailing time on weekdays and an hour or more ahead of time on weekends and holidays. Departure times are not frequent enough to take the chance of missing a boat. (Walk-on passengers and bicyclists can always get on.) For up-to-date information about ferry schedules, call Washington State Ferries toll free at 1-800-542-0810 or 1-800-542-7052, or (206) 464-6400 in Seattle.

The ferry ride of over an hour of scenic travel through the islands is a worthwhile experience in itself and allows time for coffee or a snack in the vessel's cafeteria. The boat touches at Lopez and Shaw before making port at Orcas.

From Vancouver, the route is south on 99 (in Canada) and I-5 (in the United States) to Burlington, then west on Highway 20 to Anacortes.

The alternative to driving is flying into Orcas via San Juan Airlines. The airport is six miles away from the resort, but resort personnel will pick up guests there within minutes of receiving a call. Three flights a day are scheduled from Seattle-Tacoma Airport, seven on weekends. Three daily flights leave year-round from Bellingham. Call the airline at (206) 625-9116 in Seattle, or at (206) 734-8087 in Bellingham to check flight times and arrange reservations.

Accommodations

Rosario Resort has a variety of accommodations. The Haciendas are the newest and nicest rooms, each of which has a sound-view balcony. Many suites are available, some with fireplaces, and all with adjacent parking.

The Villa units also have outside balconies, but some have superior views of the water and consequently are priced higher. The advantage of the Villas is their proximity to the lodge and its swimming pool, dining facilities, bar, Jacuzzi, and sauna.

The main lodge has only a few rooms. They are older but comfortable, and range considerably in size and price.

Then there is the Boatel, which is part of the original estate but has been completely remodeled inside expressly for the convenience of boaters wishing to spend a night ashore. The rates are lowest here.

Rosario has several different rate seasons and often has special "package plans" for considerably lower prices. Be sure to ask the

Marina and Boatel from Rosario Villas

reservations clerk for information about what is currently available.

Activities

Once you have appreciated the scenic beauty of Rosario, many other diversions are available. Without leaving the grounds, you can engage in a variety of physical activities. There are three swimming pools. One is a family pool staffed by life guards through the summer season until 1 October. Adjacent to the mansion is an adult pool perched on a cliff overhanging Cascade Bay. This pool is heated through summer until 1 November, after which avid swimmers must use the old-fashioned indoor tank pool. Whether you swim or not, you probably will enjoy steeping in the large Jacuzzi or the sauna in the lower level of the main lodge, so do not forget your swimsuits.

Rosario has an extensive beach to roam, and rents boats for salmon or cod fishing (bring your own tackle) or for exploring the sound. For the serious fisherman, a charter boat is available.

A short drive from the resort buildings, tennis buffs will find two excellent hard-surfaced courts where resort guests are welcome to play without charge.

The Orcas Golf and Country Club is located on the road from the ferry landing. It is a sporty nine-hole course built over very green, rolling hills. Most players find it challenging. Coffee and sandwiches are served in the clubhouse, or weather permitting, on the big deck overlooking the course.

Moran State Park—its entrance less than a mile from Rosario—has a widespread reputation as a destination for nature enthusiasts and those who enjoy not-too-strenuous trail hiking. This heavily forested area's trails are all well marked and exceptionally beautiful. Within the park are four lakes and the summit of Mount Constitution, any one of which makes a fine destination for a day's hike.

The trail up Mount Constitution is a three-mile climb rewarded by a spectacular view of the San Juans and snow-capped Mount Baker to the east. If you can, make this climb on foot; however, a road puts the mountaintop within a half hour's drive of Rosario.

One favorite pastime of guests at Rosario is browsing in the many craft workshops in the vicinity of East Sound. Shops selling pottery, leather, handblown glass, and candles are found there.

For evening entertainment during the summer, there is dinner-dancing to live music nightly in the Discovery House. During the off-season, entertainment is limited to Friday and Saturday evenings, either in the Discovery House or the Orcas Dining Room. Piano music is played Wednesday through Sunday year-round in the main dining room.

Rosario pool overlooking Cascade Bay

Dining

The main dining area at Rosario Resort is the Orcas Room, a cavernous room arranged on five levels to afford a 180-degree view of Cascade Bay from all the tables. It is open for meals throughout the day, year-round. This huge room hums with activity during the busy season, and the manager most skillfully handles the smaller off-season crowds by seating diners on the lower level only, close to the music and dance floor. Casual clothes are perfectly in order for almost everything at Rosario, but for dinner and dancing in the evening and for major holiday meals, women may feel more comfortable in dresses, men in jackets.

The menu contains a good variety of appealing entrées, prices are moderate, and meals are nicely served. The chef is not averse to preparing special dishes, if given a little notice. Cod are plentiful right off the resort and a specialty of the house is deep-fried, flaky white cod with coleslaw and sourdough bread. Add a bottle of dry white wine for the ultimate in gourmet dining!

Discovery House is a separate restaurant in a more recently constructed building. It has large decks for outdoor eating and is right on the water's edge about two hundred yards around the end of the bay from the lodge. Charcoal-broiled dinners are the specialty. In the wintertime Discovery House is used mostly for conventions.

Adjacent to the family pool is a building known as the Surfsider, which contains a small store for the purchase of necessities and an informal breakfast and luncheon restaurant. Breakfasts are particularly good here, and reasonably priced. In the main lodge, the Vista Cocktail Lounge serves a limited selection of deli-type sandwiches in the lounge and outside around the swimming pool.

For variety, there are several specialty restaurants in Eastsound—just ten minutes away. Most of these are small, intimate, and family operated. One of them, La Famiglia Pizzeria, serves authentic Italian food. Another, Bilbo's Kitchen, specializes in excellent Mexican food. The latter is open for dinner only and is located in an interesting tiny house in the heart of Eastsound village—well worth the trip in from the resort just to see the place. Christina's, also in Eastsound, specializes in French cuisine, and The Bungalow, on the main street of town, specializes in delicatessen food and is especially popular with the local population. For those with the leisure and the desire to see more of the island, a drive to Deer Harbor can conclude with a dinner at Otterstedt's, another family restaurant, which is known for good continental cuisine. It is open for dinner only and has a full bar.

All of these local restaurants are apt to close from time to time during the winter, and it is wise to check about them with the staff at Rosario.

The Islander Lopez Resort

Distances:

From Seattle—76 miles to Anacortes, plus ferry; allow 3 hours

From Portland—256 miles to Anacortes, plus ferry; allow 6 hours

From Vancouver, B.C.—94 miles to Anacortes, plus ferry; allow
3½ hours

Features:

Boatel facilities on sheltered bay with good moorage; quiet and
restful

Activities:

Beachcombing, bicycling, fishing, bird watching, swimming,
scuba diving, use of Jacuzzi, golf nearby

Seasons:

Year-round

Rates:

$41 to $55 for two people

Address:

Fisherman Bay, Lopez, Washington, 98261, U.S.A.

Phone:

(206) 468-2233

Marine approach to Islander Lopez

In 1974 Florence and Bill Burke made a visit to Lopez Island in the San Juans, where they saw for the first time a run-down resort on beautiful Fisherman Bay. They bought it on an impulse, and turned it into a first-class resort along seven hundred feet of tranquil waterfront. The owners since 1980 have been Bill and Stephanie Morrissey and Dean and Carolyn Jacobsen.

The main building of the Islander Lopez is a lodge that stretches along this waterfront. A long dock extends straight out from the building, providing facilities for boaters and almost fifty slips for overnight moorage. The resort is a haven for parties cruising the islands and looking for a hot bath, a big bed, and gourmet dining ashore. It is equally appealing to landlubbers who do their boating by ferry. Consequently, it is always busy in the summer.

During the winter, boating traffic slacks off and the atmosphere is more quiet—ideal for the getaway vacationer. But at times the resort still hums with activity because the owners sponsor art and photography workshops. Prominent craftsmen teach classes, which always fill up quickly, for intensive five-day stints. These workshops create a stimulating atmosphere for the resort's other guests, many of whom return later to participate in one of the classes themselves.

Routes and Distances

To get to Lopez Island, take the Anacortes ferry (see "Routes and

Distances" in Rosario Resort section). Lopez Island is the first stop on the ferry's route. Those arriving on foot can call the Islander, and a van promptly will pick them up at the landing. It is a four-mile drive to the lodge.

San Juan Airlines flies to Lopez as well as to Orcas from Seattle-Tacoma Airport. Ten flights daily are scheduled during the summer, five during the winter; the trip takes about an hour. The Islander van will pick up air travelers on call at the Lopez airport, which is only two miles from the resort.

Accommodations

The Islander lodge houses the dining room and social area and the Teredo Lounge. A big deck overlooks the bay. Two separate structures, set back from and slightly higher than the lodge, accommodate overnight guests. Each unit has an unobstructed view of the water and a large veranda from which to enjoy it. The units are large, nicely furnished, and comfortable. Eight of the units are studio kitchenettes, which (if desired) should be requested when reservations are made.

Between the lodge and the separately housed guest rooms is a circular structure housing the swimming pool, the Jacuzzi, and a meeting room where the workshops are held. The swimming pool is heated only in the summer season, but the Jacuzzi operates at all times.

Heavy summertime boat traffic makes it necessary to reserve rooms well in advance for June through September vacations. During the off-season, a call just a day or two ahead will often result in getting the room of your choice, especially for a midweek stay. Overnight moorage rates vary, depending on the season.

Activities

The central location of the Islander Lopez makes it the perfect headquarters from which to explore this interesting, tranquil island. Long walks on country roads are the best way to catch the island's farming-community flavor. The road around Fisherman Bay is a pleasant beginning, and one that can turn into an exciting adventure for sharp-eyed bird watchers.

Beachcombing is possible all around the island. Spencer Spit State Park on the east side is one favorite hunting ground. The spit juts into Rosario Strait and serves as a natural trap for floating driftwood. Over the years the winter storms have piled flotsam in an enormous jumbled pile along its length. Children love to clamber over and through the smooth, tangled logs while their elders search out interesting shapes to take home. Beyond the walls of logs are wide

Exploring Spencer Spit on Lopez Island

beaches beckoning waterfront hikers and, in warm weather, waders and a few hardy swimmers.

A way to see even more of this island is by bicycle. Lopez has a population of fewer than eight hundred permanent residents, which means that auto traffic is light. Motorists are friendly—they even wave at passing cyclists. Many miles of blacktop roads and not too many hills make cycling easy.

The clear and clean waters surrounding Lopez are particularly good for scuba diving and underwater beachcombing for those who come equipped. Kicker boat rentals are available next door at the Islander's Marine Center. A nine-hole public golf course is located near the airport.

Live entertainment is provided in the Teredo Room seven evenings a week during the busy season and on Fridays and Saturdays in the wintertime.

Lopez Island offers a variety of activities, but there are no rental equipment stores. Be sure to come well equipped for whatever you want to do.

Dining

There are four places to eat out on Lopez Island: the Islander itself, Mackaye Harbor Inn, the Galley, and the Bakery.

The main lodge of the Islander is divided into a number of separate eating areas. Dinners here are excellent, with seafood the specialty and thick steaks high on the list of favorites. The house specialty is poached baby salmon, which comes fresh daily from a pioneering salmon farm located in one of the bays on Lopez Island.

Mackaye Harbor Inn is a small restaurant in an old colonial house. It is located at the south end of the island and has a reputation for excellent home-cooked meals.

The Galley is just a short distance from the Islander. It has its own dock, as a convenience to boaters, and is a favorite with the local population. The menu is something to behold—eight pages long!—the food is good and hearty, and it is fun to have a drink at the bar and watch the panoramic sunset through the big windows facing the line of barstools.

The Bakery, half a mile from the resort, is for breakfast. Huge, succulent cinnamon rolls are served—hot from the ovens—with good, hot coffee. It is worth the walk to try them.

Sudden Valley

Distances:

From Seattle—75 miles; allow 1¾ hours

From Portland—250 miles; allow 5 hours

From Vancouver, B.C.—45 miles; allow 1¼ hours

Features:

Huge, complete condominium development on the shore of Lake
Whatcom

Activities:

Golf, tennis, nature trails, swimming, fishing, picnicking, boating and canoeing, ice skating and skiing in the winter

Seasons:

Year-round

Rates:

$40 to $60 for two people in winter, $50 to $75 for two people in
summer

Address:

Box 100, Sudden Valley, Bellingham, Washington 98226, U.S.A.

Phone:

(206) 734-6430

Sudden Valley architecture blends with nature

Sudden Valley is a huge planned resort community of some eighteen hundred acres. It adopted the motto "Where man lives with nature and both thrive," and implements it by developing the property with great care to preserve the natural characteristics of the heavily wooded hills and valleys bordering on charming Lake Whatcom. All power and utility lines are underground and out of sight here, the roads wind and ramble, buildings are designed to blend with the scenery, and the lake shore and marshlands are largely undisturbed in order to provide habitat for wild creatures.

The most surprising thing about Sudden Valley is how little it is known to Americans hailing from anywhere south of Bellingham. Canadians know it far better, and the blue-and-white license plates of British Columbia are everywhere in evidence, no doubt because it is less than an hour's drive from the border.

The focus of the development—and where getaway vacationers first check in—is the big, low, award-winning clubhouse containing the offices and restaurant facilities. Close by, in a thick grove of tall cedars and firs, is a group of fifty modern, western-style condominiums. Overlooking a small stream and the golf fairways, these constitute the rental units available to the general public.

The balance of the development, on both sides of the main road, includes other privately owned condominiums and numerous building lots, a marina on the lake, and a great variety of recreational facilities. Moreover, there are twenty parks scattered throughout the valley, providing pleasant places to relax wherever tranquil glades or hidden beaches or tumbling water happened to provide an interesting setting.

Routes and Distances

From Seattle and Portland take Interstate 5 until you are thirteen miles north of Burlington. Turn off the freeway onto the Alger exit. Take this road straight through the first traffic light. When you get to Lake Whatcom, it forks and becomes Lake Whatcom Boulevard. Take the left fork and continue on it for ten miles. If you see signs announcing the "Steam Train," you are on the correct road. Sudden Valley will appear on the right.

On the trip to or from Seattle and Portland, you might like to take a break in Marysville, a small community a few miles north of Everett. Here, within a block of each other, are the Village Cafe, famous for thirty years for its superb pies, and the tasting room of the Mountain Valley Winery. The pie and coffee combination speaks for itself; the winery is unusual and worth the stop because it specializes in fermenting a new dry wine made from raspberries, currants, loganberries, gooseberries, and other locally grown fruit. Fruit wine is not new, but dry fruit wine is, and wine enthusiasts will enjoy sampling it.

Starting from Vancouver, get to Sudden Valley by taking Canada 99 to the border and I-5 from the border south to Bellingham. Here, at the Lakeway exit, turn left to pass under the freeway overpass. Continue on Lakeway Drive for three miles, keeping to the left where the road divides. Follow the road to the end of Cable Street, then take a right on Lake Whatcom Boulevard, and continue to the golf course on the left. Look for the Sudden Valley Golf and Country Club sign. The front desk for rental units is in the clubhouse.

Accommodations

The rental units are located conveniently near the golf course, tennis courts, a swimming pool, and other centers of activity, as well as the clubhouse. With very tall trees towering over them, the three-story structures do not seem tall at all. Their architecture is typically Northwest, with rough wood exterior siding, steeply pitched roof lines, and much naturally finished woodwork inside.

There are just two basic apartment designs. Units on the first two levels are studio apartments. Third-floor units are studio lofts. The only difference between these is that the studio lofts have a bedroom and bath tucked under a sloping roof. Otherwise, each unit includes a couch that converts into a bed, a full kitchen (with dishwasher and disposal), and a private deck. Some but not all of the loft units have free-standing fireplaces, which should be specifically requested, if desired. All units have color television—"on the cable" for good reception.

Either the studios or the studio lofts are comfortable for a couple, and two couples can share a studio loft. Many getaway vacationers travel without children—getting away from it all being a frequent reason for the trip. However, there are occasions when you would like to take the children along, and Sudden Valley has a few two- and three-bedroom rentals when the extra space is needed.

Activities

Years ago Sudden Valley was a big ranch that ran a lot of cattle and horses and had three huge red barns lined up side by side on the valley floor. Now the ranch is a thing of the past, and the barns are part of the new development, converted into a recreational center. You walk to the barns from the clubhouse on a gravel path (watching out for golf balls) or drive there on a road skirting the links.

The first barn is equipped with ice-making machinery and is flooded in winter to make a skating rink for general recreation and hockey. If you come during this season, do not forget to bring ice

Golf course at Sudden Valley

skates. In summer it becomes a basketball court. The second barn is the "kiddy barn," rigged up with every playground device an active child could desire. The third barn is fitted out for teen-agers and includes a snack bar, library, game rooms, and crafts rooms.

We suspect all these facilities are provided to keep kids happy while their elders get away to play golf, for there is little doubt that the golf course is the center of attention here. Ted Robinson, who laid out the famous U.S. Open course at Pebble Beach, was the designer, and true to his reputation, it is a big, tough course, sixty-five hundred yards in length with forty-four sand traps and fifteen water hazards. It is also beautiful, nicely maintained, and a pleasure to play. In the clubhouse are men's and women's locker rooms and a fully equipped pro shop.

The six outdoor tennis courts and two swimming pools are free. The large pool, next to the barns, has racing lanes and diving, while the small one, in the adult center, is quiet and private.

There is lake swimming, too—when the water warms up—at a number of white, sandy beaches on the property. Most of these beaches have picnic tables and barbecue facilities. Boating, canoeing, and water skiing are popular on Lake Whatcom's usually calm waters.

Those who prefer to explore the land will appreciate a maze of nature trails leading through verdant fern grottos to a host of pretty little parks. At one park a boardwalk leads into a fascinating swampland. A loop trail goes to Picnic Point, a beautiful natural area with an expansive view of Lake Whatcom.

In the winter Sudden Valley provides a good base for skiing Mount Baker. The lifts and cross-country areas are approximately forty miles (fifty minutes) away.

Dining

The dining room, located in the clubhouse, features open beams and a wood-paneled ceiling sloping up to high clerestory windows. At night the lighting is soft and diffused. The windows frame views of evergreens and the golf course and there are ceiling-high folding walls that allow partitioning of the room for private parties or, when the crowd is small, for making the room more intimate. A cocktail lounge with bandstand and dance floor occupies one end of the space. It is ordinarily closed off from the dining area, but on nights when there is entertainment the music starts at nine and diners can hear it faintly through the wall. Around ten, the wall is rolled back and dinner guests finishing their meals are invited to participate in the fun.

The dining room, appropriately called the Tall Trees Room,

Tree house in a Sudden Valley park

serves all three meals seven days a week at reasonable prices. Prime rib is the dinner specialty, but there is a good variety of other dishes, including steaks, chops, chicken, and seafood. Scallops wrapped in bacon and served *en brochette* with vegetables are a favorite among the seafood specialties.

The lounge, which is also open year-round, serves no meals, but features excellent hot hors d'oeuvres, including barbecued ribs and stuffed mushrooms.

It is likely you will want to prepare some of your own meals here. Kitchens have percolators and utensils, so just bring coffee, bacon and eggs, or whatever you require.

Smuggler's Villa

Distances:
>From Seattle—87 miles, plus ferry; allow 3½ hours
>From Vancouver, B.C.—118 miles, plus ferry; allow 4 hours

Features:
>Small, secluded beach-front condominium hideaway on northern Orcas Island with comfortable, modern housekeeping units

Activities:
>Fishing, clamming, beachcombing; tennis court, pickleball court, heated swimming pool, and golf nearby

Seasons:
>Year-round; rates are higher May through September

Rates:
>Two-bedroom condominium units are $63 to $69 per night in summer, $44 in winter, for one to four occupants; add $4 per night per person for more than four

Address:
>P.O. Box 79, Eastsound, Washington 98245

Phone:
>(206) 376-2297

Mount Baker is visible from the shore near Smuggler's Villa

The San Juan Islands are well and widely known as an idyllic place to vacation. The attractions begin with the leisurely pace, beautiful scenery, and good weather, and go on to include the smell of salt air, the hypnotic sounds of waves lapping the beach and gulls crying, and a minimum of commercial activity.

Smuggler's Villa takes full advantage of all these island attributes. It is a small, compact grouping of eighteen condominiums tucked away at the very north tip of Orcas Island. It has its own beach and a long narrow boat slip to provide sheltered moorage directly alongside. Fine views of the surrounding islands and waters are the rule, as are dazzling sunsets visible from the west-facing decks.

Smuggler's Villa is one of the few places described here that does not have a restaurant of its own, but the quaint village of Eastsound, only 1.2 miles to the south, has interesting places to eat, and every condominium unit is provided with a kitchen and all utensils and accessories, so that dining is not a problem.

Because the condominiums are located at the end of the road, there are no traffic hazards to contend with and, because all the accommodations hold four people comfortably, this can be a good place to bring children. The beach is not sandy, however; it consists of dark pebbles, as do most beaches throughout the San Juans, but this doesn't keep it from being put to good use. Adults find plenty of driftwood logs to sit on, and children can hunt for unusual stones and explore the tidepools.

If you have bicycles and a rack to carry them on your car, you may want to bring them along. Bikes provide a pleasant way to get to Eastsound for supplies, and are especially good for exploring the island's back roads, byways, and neighboring resorts and beaches.

Routes and Distances

If you have your own boat, the Smuggler's Villa's moorage is a short run from Bellingham or Anacortes and you can tie up, practically at your front door, with no moorage charges to worry about.

Should you want to fly in, the Orcas Island Airport is located on an adjoining property, close enough for pilots to tie down and then walk to their villa. San Juan Airlines, flying nine-passenger Cessna airplanes, makes four flights a day to Orcas from Bellingham and five or six flights from Seattle-Tacoma Airport. (Call 622-6077 for flight information.)

If you don't come by boat or airplane, you will come via the Anacortes Ferry. There are eight ferries a day to choose from; the ride takes about an hour, usually with stops at Lopez and Shaw islands, before the ferry docks at Orcas. Be forewarned that sometimes there are long waiting lines in the busy summer months. The only answer to that is to start early and get at the head of the line. Most of the year, however, getting on board is no problem, and the trip through the maze of islands is a scenic and memorable part of a San Juan Islands vacation. The round-trip fare for car, driver, and one passenger is $18.20.

It is 10.3 miles from the Orcas ferry landing to Smuggler's Villa. Follow the main road to Eastsound Village; at the major intersection in the middle of town, go left and follow this road one mile through pleasant farm country to the Smuggler's Villa signs. You can't miss the resort.

Accommodations

There are just two styles of condominiums for rent, and the price difference between them is only six dollars in the summer; in the winter the two styles are the same price. We prefer the less expensive floor plan, although it is slightly smaller, because it is all on one level with no stairs to climb. This smaller unit has a living room-dining room, a kitchen, two bedrooms, a single bath, and a very large deck off the living room on the side facing west toward the boat moorage.

The living room has a Franklin stove in one corner, with plenty of wood and kindling in a woodbox on the deck. A sofa, matching easy chair, and coffee table are grouped in front of the fireplace. To one side is another lounge chair, and a dining table with four chairs. The kitchen is in the middle of the area, with its breakfast counter with three bar stools serving as room divider. It is a compact, handy kitchen, with everything you need for preparing meals in easy reach. It even includes a washer-dryer combination.

The two bedrooms share a single bath. The larger master bedroom has a king bed; the other is smaller with a double bed. It should be noted that the living room sofa in all units is convertible into a double bed, so that any of the condominiums can sleep six people.

The second arrangement occupies two levels, with a small bedroom and a larger loft bedroom and bath on the upper level. The downstairs living area is therefore slightly larger, which provides room for another half-bath. The washer-dryers are in the half-bath in these units, and so out of the kitchen, but that seems an unimportant difference. None of the units have telephones and only two have televisions, but whether you have a set or not is incidental, since reception in the area is not good.

As is the case for most condominium resorts, each unit is privately owned and furnished, so no two are exactly alike. The descriptions above are fairly typical, nevertheless, and all the units contain the essentials for comfortable living. For the prices charged, especially in winter, it would be difficult to find any other resort accommodations with the space, comfort, and convenience you can expect here at one of the Smuggler's Villas.

Sheltered moorage is available alongside the resort

Activities

Island living is oriented to the sea and a boat is handy to have, so many visitors trailer their boats in, making use of the launching ramp at the head of the moorage slip to put them in the water. The resort manager assigns tie-up spots at the dock to new arrivals. If you don't have a boat, several sizes of power boats are available for rent by the day or hour, also from the manager.

Fishing is good all year, particularly for salmon and cod, all around the north end of the island. It is particularly active in winter when the blackmouth salmon are in the Sound. The blackmouth are hungry, and quick to strike at this time of year. Although they are not big fish as salmon go, they make delicious eating and are probably the primary attraction for winter visitors.

Or you might want to put some pots out from the moorage dock for Dungeness crab, which are often plentiful enough so you can catch a good meal. You can also dig for steamer clams at low tide. The best place to go clamming is on the beach at the end of the country road immediately east of the resort. The resort manager is a dedicated fisherman and a good source of information about where and when to fish, crab, or go clamming.

Ordinarily the swimming pool is heated beginning May 1, although if it appears there will be an early summer, that time may be advanced a week or two. The pool season runs through September, and sometimes into October, conditions permitting. The resort's sin-

The nearby village of Eastsound lures shoppers

gle tennis court and pickleball court are situated side by side next to the pool and are usable for approximately the same period of time. The tennis court is well fenced all around and affords a nice view of the water in the direction of little Sucia Island. In the summer, sign-up sheets are posted at the tennis court gate for reserving playing times; otherwise, both courts are on a first-come-first-served basis.

When you drive up the main road from the ferry landing toward Eastsound, the Orcas Golf and Country Club's nine-hole public course comes plainly into view about three miles from Eastsound. This is a nice course—seldom crowded, fun to play, and not more than a ten-minute drive from the resort.

Other diversions for visitors here include driving over to explore Moran State Park—particularly to climb Mount Constitution, the high point of the San Juans. The chapter on Rosario Resort adds a few details about this expedition. You can also scuba dive at West Beach Resort, three miles from Smuggler's Villa. You must bring your own gear, of course, but the store at West Beach has air, and instructions about the best places to dive and what to look for.

Dining

If the fishermen in the family bring home a nice mess of fish or crab, you will, of course, use your kitchen and eat at home, probably out on the deck in nice weather. Otherwise, there are eight or nine good restaurants on the island, all worth a try.

The closest are in Eastsound. Two of these are ethnic places that are particularly popular and always busy: Bilbo's Kitchen and La Famiglia Pizzeria. The former features authentic Mexican dinners in an attractive adobe-style bungalow, with outdoor dining in its private garden courtyard. The Pizzeria, which is right next door and has recently been remodeled and enlarged, serves both lunch and dinner. Its fare is Italian, of course, and is inexpensive and good.

The Bungalow is an established restaurant in Eastsound that has recently been remodeled following a change of ownership. Lunch and dinner are served in a handsome new dining room with an outstanding view of the Sound, and a new cocktail lounge opened on the lower level shares the same views.

A newer restaurant, just a few doors down the street from The Bungalow, is Christina's, improbably located on the second floor above a service station and The Old Gaffers' Pub. It, too, overlooks the Sound from a lofty height, so that once upstairs in the spick-and-span dining room, the stores below are immaterial. Fresh seafood is the specialty, and the restaurant is building a good reputation for quality food.

One other place to eat in Eastsound is The Outlook Inn, which you encounter when first entering town from the ferry landing. Located in an imposing old white-frame building facing the main street, it is furnished in Victorian style with appropriate antiques and decoration.

The deep indentations of West Sound and East Sound divide Orcas Island into three distinct parts, with roads probing down into each part starting from the town at the island's hub. By taking the Olga Road around the left-hand side of East Sound, you can drive in about fifteen minutes to Rosario Resort, which has the island's best known and most elegant dining facilities, described here in a separate chapter. Another ten or fifteen minutes of scenic driving will take you to the little artist's colony of Olga. In the center of its mall is an interesting small restaurant, which is particularly good for a lunch stop while you inspect the arts and crafts displays of the area.

In the opposite direction from town, take the Crow Valley and Deer Harbor roads for another rewarding scenic drive around to the little community of Deer Harbor, where the Deer Harbor Inn and Otterstedt's offer two more pleasant places to eat. The Deer Harbor Inn is a new establishment in a remodeled farmhouse, with ambitious plans. Otterstedt's, just a little farther along the road, is a long-time Orcas tradition, thought by many to have the best dinners on the island. Advance reservations are usually necessary here.

Harrison Hot Springs

Distances:

From Seattle—155 miles; allow 3½ hours

From Portland—330 miles; allow 6¾ hours

From Vancouver, B.C.—82 miles; allow 1¾ hours

Features:

Majestic scenery, elegant hotel, hot-springs spa, freshwater beach

Activities:

Bathing in hot springs, easy hiking and bicycling, swimming, golf, tennis, horseback riding, evening entertainment

Seasons:

Year-round

Rates:

$50 to $90 (Canadian currency) for two people, more for individual bungalows

Address:

Harrison Hot Springs, B.C. V0M 1K0, Canada

Phone:

In Seattle toll free (206) 682-1981 or toll free (206) 622-5736; Harrison Hot Springs (604) 796-2244; Vancouver, B.C., toll free 521-8888

Entrance to Harrison Hot Springs Hotel

The setting of this long-popular Canadian resort is unsurpassed for natural beauty. Nestled at one end of Lake Harrison on a wide, sandy beach, it is ringed on all sides with snow-capped peaks and majestic vistas.

The Harrison is an old hotel that has been modernized and expanded frequently over the years. Its main attraction has always been the clear, hot, mineral water that bubbles up in a rocky cavern on the lake's shore a few hundred yards from the hotel. Early visitors bathed in the cavern itself; now the hot water is piped to the hotel's "health pavilion" where guests can soak in a 105-degree spa or a 90-degree pool and, if they like, sip the bitter waters from a special fountain.

The hotel grounds are extensive and impressively maintained. You can devote an entire afternoon to strolling the paths and lawns and enjoying the plantings, ponds, and birds. Fall is a particularly delightful time to be here because the weather is usually good and the leaves are turning color. If there is a nip in the air, it makes the hot mineral baths especially pleasant.

The little town of Harrison Hot Springs, which more or less grew up around the resort, consists mostly of a single, broad avenue that parallels the beach and is lined with shops and restaurants on the side facing the lake. Everything in this village is within easy walking distance of the hotel, which dominates the eastern end of the avenue.

Unlike so many present-day resorts, the Harrison continues to cultivate formality. It still has a staff of red-coated attendants reminiscent of empire days. And every afternoon at four a tea service is set out on white linen in the lobby, and a gracious hostess sits and serves tea with cookies and pastries to the assembled guests. It is this touch of old elegance, plus the breathtaking setting and easy accessibility to Vancouver and northern Washington cities, that has made the Harrison a favorite get-away-from-it-all retreat for vacationers who want to be waited on and pampered in a complete change of scene.

Routes and Distances

From Seattle and Portland take Interstate 5 to Bellingham. Just past Bellingham, look for the Meridian Street exit, which is Washington 539. Follow 539 to the Lynden cutoff—Washington 546—and turn left onto it. Take this road to the border crossing at Sumas. Follow the same road a few miles farther to where it runs into Trans-Canada 1. Go east on 1 to the Rosedale exit; here pick up B.C. 9 and proceed north through Agassiz to Harrison Hot Springs.

This route gives you excellent roads and much breathtaking scenery. It is also the most direct and fastest way. If extra time is available going home, from Sumas take Washington 9 all the way back to the Seattle area. You will pass through a succession of small, peaceful farmland communities and near shores of inland lakes, and you will experience what fun driving used to be before the advent of freeways.

There are two good routes to Harrison Hot Springs from Vancouver. For variety, take a different one each way. First is the excellent four-lane Trans-Canada highway through lush, mountain-rimmed farmlands. Take the Rosedale exit to B.C. 9 and Harrison. The alternative is scenic Lougheed Highway, B.C. 7, along the north shore of the Fraser River. Turn north onto B.C. 9 just before Agassiz. It is no farther than Route 1, but it takes longer.

Accommodations

Having been added to over the years, the Harrison Hotel now has 280 rooms in four different types, which range considerably in rate. The original building has been carefully maintained to retain its air of graciousness, and the accommodations in this section have a certain charm, but the plumbing and showers sometimes leave a little to be desired. For slightly more it is worthwhile to ask for a room in the Tower or West Wing, which is the most recent addition. These rooms are spacious and modern, each with its own view-balcony overlooking either the lake on one side, or the swimming pool and lawn on the other.

Across a courtyard from the main building is an annex known as the Lodge containing the least expensive rooms of the complex. Lodge rooms are comfortable and adequate, but modest in comparison with the Tower rooms.

The Bungalows are a unique feature, which old-time guests will remember for their charming settings, scattered on the lawn amongst trees and gardens. These are ideal for families and have the additional advantage of permitting pets for those who find it difficult to leave the dog at home.

The Harrison Hotel offers special rates in the off-season and also has a constantly changing variety of special package plans, which the reservations clerk is happy to explain upon inquiry.

Activities

Visitors to Harrison Hot Springs will never suffer from a lack of things to do. Year-round there are diversions for the most relaxed as well as the liveliest of guests. In summer the focal point of activity is Lake Harrison. The hotel's lawns stretch right to the beach, where sunbathing, swimming, water skiing, sailing, power boating, and long strolls on the sand or along the bordering pathways are popular.

The hotel's pleasant outdoor swimming pool is ringed with com-

Bikers enjoying Lake Harrison shoreline

fortable lounge furniture. At midday a deli-sandwich bar is set up at poolside and cocktails will be served at any time. Adjacent to it is the health pavilion with its mineral baths. Guests usually like to alternate between the hot spa water and the cooler outdoor pool. The pavilion is connected to the hotel by a covered passageway and is open year-round. (It has men's and women's massage rooms with professional attendants available for an extra charge.) There is a game room with table tennis and pool in the lower level of the hotel.

A favorite walk for hikers is on a wide, two-mile trail around the end of the lake. It goes past the mineral springs and ends at the mouth of the Harrison River. The grandeur of the snow-capped peaks reflected by the lake is a constant and much photographed view from this trail. Longer hikes can be taken up the river on less developed trails or in the vicinity of Deer and Hicks lakes, a short drive to the east. Both of these lakes are most heavily used on summer weekends. During the week you can usually enjoy swimming in solitude in their remarkably clear waters.

Trail to the hot springs at Harrison

Coming into Harrison Hot Springs from the south, you will see a nine-hole public golf course on the left about a mile before the hotel. It is nestled in a flat valley at the very foot of abruptly rising cliffs, and golfers sometimes must wait for deer to move out of the line of fire before making a next shot.

On the side lawn of the hotel are two asphalt tennis courts. Riding horses are available at a nearby stable, and the hotel also keeps about twenty bicycles on hand to rent to guests who want to explore the neighborhood streets and trails. Around the end of the lake to the right is a good paved road that you can ride for about five miles to Sasquatch Park at its end. Throughout the farmlands surrounding Harrison are many miles of utterly flat, seldom traveled country roads, which are ideal for longer rides. Most of the rental bikes are one- and three-speed models, so those who prefer a ten-speed should bring their own.

Dining

Breakfast, lunch, and dinner are served in the hotel's Copper Room—a large room with many tables attractively arranged on several levels. Here sports clothes of all types are appropriate for breakfast and luncheon. Dining is a pleasant experience in the Copper Room, and the food is good, though the prices seem moderately high.

The Terrace bar opens directly off the hotel lobby and adjoins the dining room. It features live music each night and unpredictably, just for fun, at other times in the afternoon and evening.

Those who really enjoy dressing up for an evening will have the opportunity to don their finery for dining and dancing in the Copper Room. Others, more casually inclined, may wear dressy sports attire. Elegant service, a band, dancing, and some form of entertainment are nightly features. Prices are high, but guests have a delightful time and in the summer the Copper Room is always booked to capacity.

Along the avenue, a short walk from the Harrison, are additional eating places. One of the most interesting is the Black Forest, which, as its name suggests, serves German food. The decorations are Bavarian, inside and out, and the food is uniformly excellent. Conca Doro also serves ethnic food—Italian. Traditional dishes are available (pizza, lasagna, and scallopini), but it is perhaps best appreciated for its remarkably good Caesar salads. Prices are moderate at both restaurants.

The Westin Bayshore

Distances:
>From Seattle—145 miles; allow 3 hours
>From Portland—320 miles; allow 6½ hours

Features:
An elegant city-center resort on the harbor in downtown Vancouver, B.C.

Activities:
Sight-seeing about town and in Stanley Park, waterfront strolling, cycling, jogging, swimming, and use of health club facilities

Seasons:
Year-round; special winter rates offer one-third off regular prices; advance reservations always advisable

Rates:
$105 to $135 (Canadian currency) for two people

Address:
1601 West Georgia Street, Vancouver, B.C. V6G 2V4, Canada

Phone:
(604) 682-3377; toll free in United States, 1-800-228-3000

Vancouver's Westin Bayshore

Throughout North America there are few vacation resorts that have their own saltwater marina, are right next door to miles of forested trails, and yet are at the heart of a large, cosmopolitan city. The Westin Bayshore is special, partly because of these attributes, partly because Vancouver is an exciting city, and partly because the Bayshore is an outstanding hotel.

All you have to do is look out the hotel window at the harbor below to sense the throb of world commerce and the adventure inherent in an orientation to the sea. Ships from a dozen nations are anchored in the roadsteads or moving in and out through the narrows to the Burnaby docks. Float planes, essential communication links with the remote north, circle incessantly to land and take off from the harbor. Rowers in eight-oared shells from the Vancouver Rowing Club boathouse exercise all day long. Ferries fan out in all directions, and fishing boats and private craft of every description ply the waters around the four big floating gas docks in front of the hotel.

To the right is a skyline of high-rise architecture, impressive in daytime and spectacular at night.

Getaway vacationers can check in here and stay as long as desired without ever needing an automobile. There is plenty to do, plenty to see, and a wide range of fine places to eat and drink within easy walking distance of the hotel. But you may need raincoats, because it is likely to rain at any time of year.

Around the corner, past a row of shipyards and marine repair docks, is Stanley Park. Almost as large as downtown Vancouver, it has seven miles of waterfront, still forested in old-growth timber and still populated with geese, waterfowl, and fish hawks.

Take a taxi or bus for the short ride down Burrard Inlet toward the ferry docks, where you will find the city's reconstructed, brick-paved old section, known as Gastown. It is designed for strolling and window shopping, and is full of interesting stores and eating places. Nearby is the enchantment of Chinatown.

The Bayshore itself has recently been expanded to provide indoor athletic activities as well as additional rooms and dining accommodations. The hotel offers guests many conveniences, including shops and free bus service every half hour to the downtown shopping area. And its health club is a cheerful place to exercise or relax. With all this, the Bayshore is a resort, an athletic club, and an elegant central hotel rolled into one, and available for the private use of getaway vacationers anytime they want to pick up the phone and say they are coming.

Routes and Distances

From Seattle and Portland take Interstate 5 to Canada. At the border the freeway becomes Canada 99. It goes through the Deas Tunnel under the Fraser River, across Lulu Island, and over the Oak Street Bridge into Vancouver itself. At this point, the freeway becomes a city street, with cross traffic and traffic lights. If you lose track of the route markers along it, just stay on Oak Street all the way to Twelfth Avenue; then turn left, drive five blocks to Granville Street, turn right onto Granville, cross another bridge, and continue through the downtown area to West Georgia Street. Turn left onto Georgia (where you will again see route 99 markers), and after a dozen blocks keep a lookout for the large sign marking the hotel on the right. Drive in under the porte cochere to register; then park in the big lot directly in front of the hotel. This lot is free to hotel guests. The front desk will issue your parking pass at check-in.

Accommodations

This large hotel's 520 rooms are spacious, tastefully furnished, and nicely arranged. All have separate dressing alcoves and a sitting area next to large sliding glass doors opening out to the view. The type of view is the important thing, and room rates vary accordingly. Standard rooms have a "city view," medium rooms have "harbor views," and the choice deluxe rooms on the upper floors look out over the whole panorama of city and harbor. Most rooms have twin beds and reservations will be confirmed only on that basis, though the management will try to reserve a room with a double, queen-size, or king-size bed.

Winter is a good time to plan a trip to the Westin Bayshore because rates are significantly reduced between 1 November and 1 April.

Activities

Stanley Park is an easy walk from the Bayshore and within its one thousand acres are diversions of many kinds. Any time of year in any kind of weather, strollers can be seen along the seven miles of seawall fronting the harbor—observing the changing views of the city, crossing under the high, graceful Lions Gate Bridge, passing the "girl in the wet suit" statue on its offshore rock, or watching for marine life and unusual birds.

In the park are numerous paths through wooded areas, which walkers share with cyclists and joggers. (Joggers can take the little swimming pool elevator up to their rooms in the hotel and avoid the main elevator.) One leads to the zoo and polar bears and penguins. Another leads to the extensive aquarium and daily showings of trained dolphins and killer whales. The zoo and aquarium alone deserve a full day's exploration. Other paths lead to other places: tearooms, tennis courts, pools, playfields, picnic areas, and the Vancouver Rowing Club.

Harbor from Bayshore rooms at dusk

There is no better way to get a panoramic view of the entire Vancouver area than by taking the tram ride to the top of Grouse Mountain. This magnificent view, only about twenty minutes from the hotel by car, can be enjoyed over a meal in the mountaintop chalet, and in the wintertime you can ski or watch skiers. A point of interest on the way to the skyride is the Capilano Suspension Bridge. One of the largest and highest in the world, it offers a fantastic view of the canyon and river far below, but it sways gently, and crossing it is not for the fainthearted.

Many visitors to Vancouver enjoy browsing or shopping. Gastown is often their first destination. This is the place where Vancouver began, and after years of neglect, the area has been restored and rejuvenated. Now, filled with intriguing cul-de-sacs and tiny shops and restaurants, it has an aura of mingled past and present and bustles with activity.

Two more popular browsing and shopping destinations are Granville Mall and the Robsonstrasse. The former is between Nelson and Hastings streets. The latter is a square on Robson Street at Hornby and Bute that has been remodeled to duplicate a section from a typical European village. Robson Street itself is lined with interesting specialty shops.

Dining

The dining experience plays an important part in our getaway vacations, but it is paramount when the getaway is in the heart of a big city. There we are in the mood to dress up, go out on the town, and enjoy being pampered and entertained during a leisurely cocktail hour and dinner.

Guests of the Bayshore need never leave the hotel premises to enjoy such evenings. One of the hotel's notable features is that Trader Vic's world-renowned restaurant connects to the hotel lobby through a breezeway. The restaurant is divided into a number of intimate areas decorated with nautical artifacts. The menu is enormous, featuring selections from the cuisine of many countries, and the service is impeccable. Guests should leave Trader Vic's feeling they have chosen well for a night on the town.

The Garden Restaurant is another delightful dining area. Located on the main level adjacent to the lobby, it looks out on the pool and the surrounding landscaping, and is filled with plants and lattice-work to create a pleasant indoor–outdoor atmosphere. Breakfast, lunch, and dinner are served daily, but on Sunday it is most famous for its elegant brunch served between 10 A.M. and 2 P.M. including fresh salmon, sautéed chicken livers, cold cuts, cheeses, fresh fruits, and a particularly noteworthy French toast. The price is

Suspension bridge popular outing for Bayshore visitors

reasonable and the brunch attracts people from all over town, the usual attendance on any given Sunday running between eight hundred and one thousand.

There are also three lounges in the hotel in which to enjoy an after-dinner drink and prolong the evening. The Garden Lounge overlooks the marina and features live music nightly except on Sundays. The Marine Lounge is a good vantage point from which to view the harbor and city lights at night; it is open for dancing from 9 P.M. to 2 A.M. The Harbour Bar at Trader Vic's, with a spectacular panoramic view of the city and harbor, has become *the* place people meet in Vancouver.

Outside the hotel but within easy walking distance are a number of interesting restaurants. One of them, Mother Tucker's Food Experience, is a popular place on Alberni Street and has a rustic, farmlike atmosphere and reasonable dinner prices. It features a hearty prime-rib dinner, a salad bar, and homemade bread and pastries. Since no reservations are taken, be sure to arrive early, and expect to wait.

Also nearby, but far removed from the rollicking mood of Mother Tucker's, is the small, intimate French restaurant, Lili La Puce— very expensive, but very nice.

Humphreys, high atop the Denman Place Inn on Comax Street, is the ultimate for view watchers. Thirty-five stories up, the dining room and the bar share a panoramic view of the harbor, the coastal mountains, and the city.

Although Gastown is not within walking distance, it is a short trip by car or taxi and should not be ignored for dining and nighttime activity. For both lunch and dinner, it is full of enjoyable places, such as the Old Spaghetti Factory on Water Street. Where else can you eat spaghetti on a 1910 British Columbia electric railway car in the middle of an old warehouse furnished with antiques?

Frisbee's, located in another old rail car, specializes in stroganoff crepes. Other places we suggest trying are Brother John's next door, the Noodle Maker, the Jade Palace, Onon (said to be a favorite of former premier Pierre Trudeau), and the Hoho Inn.

Island Hall Hotel

Distances:
From Seattle—183 miles, plus ferry; allow 6 hours
From Portland—358 miles, plus ferry; allow 9½ hours
From Vancouver, B.C.—35 miles, plus ferry; allow 3 hours

Features:
Traditional old beach resort; slow paced, family oriented

Activities:
Swimming, beach activities, croquet, tennis, short driving trips,
stream fishing, hiking, snow skiing

Seasons:
Year-round; reservations should be made as well in advance as
possible for holidays and summer weekends

Rates:
$42 to $62 (Canadian currency) for two people

Address:
P.O. Box 340, Parksville, B.C. V0R 2S0, Canada

Phone:
(604) 248-3225; in Vancouver 681-3800

Main lodge at Island Hall Hotel

Southeast Vancouver Island, between Duncan and the Campbell River, has long been a summer-vacation favorite with Canadians. Almost midway up the Strait of Georgia is Parksville, and in the center of Parksville lies the big, sprawling Island Hall Hotel, the oldest and most fondly known resort on the inside coast.

The hotel grounds occupy ten acres of prime waterfront on the inside curve of a shallow, sandy bay. In front of the dignified old lodge, broad lawns and formal gardens sweep down to the water's edge. Construction began in the early 1920s, and everything about the hotel reflects age and tradition. Furnishing and decor, accordingly, are not always in the most modern style, and there are occasional details of equipment and maintenance that might seem to need up-dating. But you sense that here tradition is easily offended and change, when it comes, must be gradual and carefully executed. Meanwhile, the aura of elegance past remains a definite part of the charm and appeal of Island Hall, and it invites you to relax at this unusual resort.

Routes and Distances

From Seattle and Portland follow Interstate 5 to customs at Blaine. On the Canadian side of the border, the route becomes 99; take it (not 99A, which goes through New Westminster, an unnecessary diversion) to Vancouver.

From Vancouver go north on 99 through Stanley Park and across the Lions Gate Bridge. Trans-Canada 1 joins 99 in North Vancouver and leads directly to Horseshoe Bay. Ferry departures are from the Horseshoe Bay terminal.

As the crow flies, Parksville is only fifty-five miles from downtown Vancouver, a relatively short trip. But the ferry ride across the Strait of Georgia takes almost two hours, and you must expect to wait in line for the ferry. Call the British Columbia ferry system in Vancouver at (604) 669-1211 for up-to-date information about fares and schedules. These ferries have good cafeterias, and one way to make the trip seem shorter is to have lunch aboard (bring your own wine if you like). Pack a book to read, and the wait and crossing can be a relaxing break in the total journey.

From the ferry terminal at Nanaimo take B.C. 19 for twenty-two miles to Parksville. The hotel, on the highway to the right, is at the center of town and is well marked.

Accommodations

Most of the rooms at Island Hall are very large, built with families in mind. Scattered among lawns and gardens are seven annexes containing a total of seventy-four guest rooms; each annex is named after a member of the founder's family. A typical room contains two double beds separated from a sitting area by bookcases, and includes a television, a narrow porch on the ocean side, and a covered veranda. The whole room, including the open-beam ceiling, is paneled in dark, knotty cedar, accentuating the old-fashioned, country-lodge atmosphere. The lodge itself has more guest rooms.

The separate annexes and the main lodge all offer some choice of bed combinations: doubles, singles, and hideaway beds. Prices are slightly higher for the annexes than for the main lodge, which in turn has higher prices on the water than on the highway side.

In the summer old-timers return to Island Hall like swallows, so reservations should be made well in advance. On Thanksgiving, Christmas, New Year's Day, and Easter there are parties, banquets, and other popular events, which also require early reservations. Other winter reservations can be obtained on short notice.

Activities

The Island Hall property is situated right at the apex of Parksville Bay and includes over one thousand feet of white, sandy beach. At low tide you can walk out on it for nearly a mile.

As might be expected, summertime activity centers around this vast stretch of sand. Sunbathing, dabbling in the tide pools, building sand castles, and swimming (when the tide comes in) are popular. If

Wading in the surf

you enjoy raw oysters, bring a bucket or sack, an oyster knife, and some tabasco sauce, and gather your oysters here. In the evening, beachside barbecues are popular.

Elsewhere on the property guests play tennis on two asphalt courts or play croquet on the lawn. Croquet, in fact, is not taken lightly in these parts; the world championships are played here in August, and hotel guests may enter the eliminations. The resort also has a greenhouse, an indoor swimming pool and exercise room, a large convention hall, and an outdoor barbecue.

Inland, there are trout streams to fish, caves to explore at Horne Lake, the famous Cathedral Grove forest sanctuary to visit, a scenic trail up to Little Mountain lookout to climb, and ancient petroglyphs to discover off the Allsbrook Road; and these are just a few of the outing possibilities within a short driving distance of the hotel. In winter the indoor pool and exercise room get a lot of use.

Skiing is only thirty minutes away at Mount Arrowsmith, which is a full-service facility with lodge, restaurant, licensed premises, chair lift, T bars, and rope tows. Near Courtenay, about a ninety-minute drive away, is another ski area, with the imposing name of Forbidden Plateau. Skiers like to check in at Island Hall on Friday night to ski Forbidden on Saturday, Arrowsmith on Sunday, and return home Sunday evening. You can lose the chill of the slopes in a big, separate Jacuzzi located in an alcove off the swimming pool.

In the evening, you may enjoy a visit to the Frontiersman pub near Coombs or the hotel's own pub, which has live music for dancing.

Dining

A good plan for the first night at Island Hall is to make a reservation for dinner and try out the hotel's recently renovated and redecorated Georgia Restaurant. Food is served by candlelight in a relaxing decor of green and coral colors with rattan furniture and exotic plants. Big windows facing the waterfront provide nice views of the beach and mainland mountains. Canadian tax policy promotes domestic wines by making them cheaper than imports, so this is a good opportunity to sample wines from the upper Okanogan Valley. Some of them are good and very inexpensive.

Informal dining is available upstairs in the Coffee Garden. As its name implies, it is a coffee shop, open daily for all three meals.

There are two other good places for dinner in the area. One is the Coach and Horses about six miles away. Take the Island Highway south just past the weigh station and turn left on Northwest Bay Road. After you have gone about three miles—just when it seems this must be the wrong road—look for a little sign on the right. Drive in and find a charming British pub crowded with people having a good time. Quite an amazing find in the middle of nowhere! It serves a limited selection of good, traditionally British food such as roast beef with Yorkshire pudding and steak-and-kidneys. Prices are reasonable.

The second is Ma Maison, situated in a remodeled waterfront house on the right-hand side of the road to the north about one-half mile from the hotel. It specializes in French cuisine and wines and is quite good. Reservations are usually necessary and can be obtained by calling (604) 248-5859.

The Empress Hotel

Distances:

From Seattle—via *Princess Marguerite*, 4½-hour cruise; via ferry, 76 miles to Anacortes, plus ferry, allow 6 hours

From Portland—238 miles to Port Angeles and car ferry *Coho* to Victoria, allow 6½ hours

From Vancouver, B.C.—41 miles plus Tsawwassen ferry, allow 3½ hours

Features:

Charming, old-world hotel; delightful "city of gardens," with maritime orientation; full of quaint shops and winding streets

Activities:

Sight-seeing, shopping, museums, exhibits, antique hunting— all within easy walking distance of the hotel

Seasons:

Year-round

Rates:

$80 to $100 (Canadian currency) for two people May through October; approximately 25% less during winter months (except holidays)

Address:

721 Government Street, Victoria, B.C. V8W 1W5, Canada

Phone:

(604) 384-8111; toll free in United States, 1-800-828-7447; toll free in British Columbia, 112-899-268-9411

Majestic Empress Hotel across the Inner Harbour

Victoria, B.C., is by almost any measure one of North America's most rewarding cities for visitors to explore and enjoy. It exudes English charm and tradition at every turn, yet time and again as you move about the city you encounter reminders of the rich Northwest Indian cultures, and of bawdy frontier days when the fur trade, fisheries, and lumberjacking made up Victoria's economic framework.

The city is compact and easy to find your way around in. You can do most of your exploring on foot, making sight-seeing a relaxed and pleasant experience. The Empress Hotel is at the very heart of the areas of major interest. When you arrive in Victoria, all routes lead to the harbor front, where it is impossible to miss the elegant old hotel, which for over seventy years has remained the traditional host to royalty, prime ministers, and other dignitaries visiting British Columbia. The huge, sedate, ivy-covered structure, set among lawns and formal gardens, dominates the head of Victoria Harbour. To its left are the equally venerable and stately buildings of the Provincial Parliament and the Provincial Museum. To the right extend Douglas, Government, and Wharf streets, jammed with import shops, boutiques, restaurants, and malls.

The big surprise to first-time visitors who know the hotel's age and history is discovering how well preserved and spritely the old girl remains. Mementos of empire are in evidence throughout the hotel.

The walls are adorned with prints of British troops in action on the old frontiers. In the Bengal Room the waiters wear East Indian costumes, and a tiger skin dominates the mantle at the end of the large room. This, by the way, is "everyone's bar" in Victoria and a favorite businessman's lunching place. It is said that if a person has acquaintances, he will surely meet at least one of them here, sooner or later.

The intimate little Library bar adjoining the lobby is a favorite meeting place for tête-à-tête conversation, and when Parliament is in session many significant political deals are transacted here.

The lobby itself seems cavernous because of its high ceilings. It is almost always abuzz with activity, especially in the afternoon, when high tea is served, complete with the traditional crumpets, cakes, and sandwiches.

The Empress prides itself on being a very personalized hotel. Most of its guests are expected to return again, some of them year after year. When they do so they are delighted to find themselves remembered and greeted by name. Anyone staying more than a few days, in fact, is soon known to key employees, who go out of their way to show little personal attentions. This is the deliberate spirit of the Empress, and a major reason it qualifies as one of North America's great hotels.

Routes and Distances

A brief sea voyage will take you from the mainland to Victoria, at the tip of Vancouver Island. There are four carriers to choose from: the venerable *Princess Marguerite* from Seattle, the state ferry from Anacortes, the car ferry *Coho* from Port Angeles, and the Tsawwassen ferry from Vancouver.

From Seattle a cruise on the *Princess Marguerite* is a pleasant way to get to Victoria. She leaves from her downtown berth at Pier 69 at 8 A.M.—May through October—and arrives in Victoria at 12:15 P.M., just in time for lunch. She heads back to Seattle at 5:30 P.M. Round-trip fare for walk-on passengers is $29, no reservations required. Because many people take the *Marguerite* on one-day excursions, the boat is sometimes too crowded for comfort. Seasoned travelers, therefore, advise spending a few extra dollars to rent a private state-room. The state-rooms all open conveniently onto the main deck, and passengers having one are assured of a place to read, play bridge, or just stretch out in comfort when they wish. Reservations and state-rooms may be obtained by phoning (206) 623-5560 in Seattle.

A delightful cruise through the San Juan Islands is afforded by the daily Washington State Ferry run from Anacortes to Sidney. Unfortunately, the boat leaves Anacortes early in the morning,

The M.V. Coho *arrives daily in Victoria from Port Angeles*

which means people traveling from Seattle must get up even earlier. The trip takes four hours. (Schedule and fare information are available from Washington State Ferries: statewide toll free, 1-800-542-0810.) You then must drive from Sidney to Victoria.

Portland is a long way from Victoria, but do make the trip if you can find time. Portlanders can drive to Anacortes and take the state ferry, as above, or they can drive U.S. 101 to Port Angeles, leave the car there (or not, as they please), and take Black Ball's M.V. *Coho* across the Strait of Juan de Fuca to Victoria. Before the Hood Canal Bridge sank, this ferry to Victoria was popular with Seattle travelers. Until it is rebuilt, other routes will now be preferable. During the winter the *Coho* leaves each morning and returns each afternoon. The schedule is expanded in the spring to three round trips and later, at the peak of the season, to four. Call (206) 622-2222 in Seattle or (206) 457-4491 in Port Angeles for information. At Victoria the *Coho* docks directly in front of the *Princess Marguerite*, just a five-minute walk from the Empress.

From Vancouver it is just a short drive south on 99 and then B.C. 17 to Tsawwassen, where ferries leave every two hours for the run to Swartz Bay near Sidney. The ferry ride takes under two hours, but travelers should realize that summer traffic is heavy and there are long waiting lines at the terminal. In Vancouver call (604) 669-1211 for information about sailing times.

Accommodations

No matter which room you are assigned at the Empress, you can count on comparative spaciousness and a touch of elegance. The halls alone in this grand old place are wider than the rooms found in some of the more modern hotels. The large rooms, combined with excellent room service, make informal hosting convenient and pleasant for you.

The windows, it is true, have old-fashioned wood sashes and the bathroom fixtures are dated, but maintenance is meticulous and, old or not, things work as they should. Moreover, new is combined with old where it counts. Headboards are antiques, but bedsprings, mattresses, and upholstery are modern and comfortable. Still, it is the airy, high ceilings, the paneling, and the beautifully preserved old furnishings that we most remember and appreciate.

The hotel has a few large suites. Otherwise, there are three other types of accommodations, which vary in price only according to size, how high up in the hotel they are located, and the views they afford. The nicest rooms, the "deluxe," are on the upper floors, overlooking the myriad of harbor activities. The "superior" rooms are in the mid-section of the hotel where the view is less spectacular, and the "standard" rooms, the least expensive, are on the lower levels of the hotel. They are smaller and offer a minimal view. All of the accommodations offer the same fine quality furnishings and a choice of bed sizes.

The Empress offers a variety of package plans, mini-holidays, music festivals, and other special events, some of which may fit into a getaway vacationer's plans. As these are always changing, up-to-date information should be obtained by writing or phoning the hotel. Reservations at these times should be made well in advance.

Activities

In Victoria the name of the game is sight-seeing and shopping and a lot of walking, so bring clothing suitable for town use, and include sweaters and windbreakers for the chilly waterfront. Within a radius of just a few blocks of the Empress are enough things to do and see to occupy weeks of time and still not cover them all.

Sight-seeing usually begins with the Provincial Museum, near the Empress on Belleville Street. There is a saying that even the most adamant museum evader will forget any antipathies here. Start on the third floor and allow lots of time. A few hours can flee quite unexpectedly while you roam through the lifelike displays showing the heritage and environment of British Columbia since its earlier days. Dramatic re-creations of lumber camps, sawmills, deep-rock mines, salmon canneries, saloons, and farms make a vivid impression of Canada's formative years. Perhaps most impressive of all is the incredible exhibit of totem poles and other Canadian art.

A display in the same vein is on the ground floor of the hotel itself, opposite the main entrance. This is the Miniature World display. Tiny, exquisitely detailed figures enliven over twenty authentic settings, representing famous battles, classic scenes from literature, and interpretations of well-known fairy tales. The most interesting and best displayed is a panoramic history of the Canadian Pacific Railroad during the thirty years of its construction at the turn of the century. It is an incredible re-creation of time and space, 110 feet long, that took five artists over a year and a half to construct.

There are other interesting exhibits to see within a block of the hotel. Across Douglas Street is the nostalgic Classic Car Museum, a million-dollar exhibit of rare cars—from Model-T Fords to Rolls Royces—some additionally distinguished by the queens, prime ministers, and presidents who rode in them.

Around the block on Belleville Street is Tussaud's Royal London Wax Museum, filled with life-size wax figures of famous British and American personages. Directly below it the Undersea Gardens extend into the harbor. Visitors descend below water level here to observe, through watertight windows, sea creatures in their natural habitat.

Daily during the summer season, fourteen different Greyline bus tours leave the hotel to take visitors to more distant places of interest, such as the world-famous Butchart Gardens and the panoramic Marina Drive. First-timers are well advised to take the short Grand City Tour soon after arrival in Victoria to obtain an overview and general orientation to the area.

A shopping expedition in Victoria might take you on a leisurely stroll along Government Street. From this main thoroughfare you can explore interesting side streets and squares for the many imported goods and native crafts available in fascinating shops.

Turn right from Government onto Fort Street to find the antique shops, which deserve special mention. Victoria is the antique capital of Canada, possibly because a great many of Victoria's original settlers came directly from England around Cape Horn by sailing ship, bringing all their fine, old-world furniture with them. To the delight of modern-day treasure hunters, a steady stream of these heirlooms is now finding its way into the shops.

Those who avoid sight-seeing and shopping might like to try one of the several nearby public golf courses or visit Beacon Hill Park and its five miles of waterfront paths. One end of the park is only a little over a block from the hotel.

Something is usually going on at the McPherson Playhouse Performing Arts Center on Centennial Square. See if you can catch a free concert at noon, then find out about the evening's program. McPherson's offers musicals, drama, ballet, and occasionally, arts and crafts exhibits.

For evening activities there are theaters, movies, and nightclubs all about town; most are within easy walking distance of the hotel.

Dining

A cheerful place to start the day is in the hotel's bustling Garden Cafe, which opens at seven-thirty. It is known for its good breakfasts, which are served fast and piping hot by attentive help who never allow the coffee to cool in your cup. You may eat lunch here, too, but you are likely to choose the Bengal Room or the Library Bar instead. The Bengal Room hums with activity at noon and the menu consists of two dishes: a popular curry, different every day, and one other specialty. Such a limited menu greatly expedites service to the large crowd that gathers.

Luncheon in the Library is quite different. This small, richly paneled room features comfortable overstuffed furniture and small, low tables grouped around a fireplace, which always has a fire burning in the winter. It has a small bar in front of leaded windows, and in the corner by the bookcases a chef in a white cap carves from a baron of beef and prepares the food orders. The atmosphere is quiet and intimate here and the food is excellent.

Dinner is served formally at the Empress in the Victorian Dining Room, where the menu is extensive. Thursday and Sunday night buffets are more casual. They present an elegant and tempting array of salads, numerous entrées, and a beautiful display of pastries and desserts. As might be expected, these buffets are less expensive than the regular dinner.

It is quite possible to eat all your meals in the hotel and have good food at every one. On the other hand, being a town that thrives on tourism, Victoria is filled with restaurants offering a wide selection of interesting food, and it is fun to try something different. One of the best places to go, noted particularly for excellent seafood, is Chauney's on Humbolt Street. The atmosphere is warm and inviting and the prices reasonable.

Laurel Point Inn

Distances:

From Seattle—via *Princess Marguerite*, 4¼-hour cruise; via ferry, 76 miles to Anacortes, plus ferry, allow 6 hours

From Portland—via *Coho*, 238 miles to Port Angeles, plus ferry, allow 6½ hours

From Vancouver, B.C.—via Tsawwassen ferry, 41 miles driving, plus ferry, allow 3½ hours

Features:

New resort hotel, surrounded by water and the activity of Victoria's harbor; within walking distance of downtown; probably mildest weather in Canada

Activities:

Walking, bicycling, tennis, swimming, sight-seeing, browsing, shopping, antique hunting

Seasons:

Year-round

Rates:

$69 to $82 (Canadian currency) for double occupancy, year-round

Address:

680 Montreal Street, Victoria, B.C. V8V 1Z8, Canada

Phone:

(604) 386-8721; toll free in British Columbia, 112-800-663-3397

Victoria's Laurel Point Inn

The Delta chain of Canadian inns constructs its hotels on the outskirts of cities—close enough to accommodate business trade, but far enough away to offer the luxury and amenities of a resort and thus attract vacation-oriented clientele.

As the capital of British Columbia, Victoria deals in government, so the commercial trade at Laurel Point includes a high percentage of politicians and government employees. Even in normally slack vacation season, the lobby, dining room, and lounge bustle with people and activity always so vital to the enjoyment of a hotel by its guests.

Laurel Point itself is a wedge of land that juts into the bay to form Victoria's Inner Harbour. The inn, at the apex of the point, has water on two sides, and its modernistic architecture employs a staggered arrangement of rooms so that every room has a harbor view and catches the summer breeze on warm evenings.

Victoria itself is unique in so many ways. The most "English" of all Canadian cities, it has traditional double-decker buses plying the streets and is replete with museums and replicas of old buildings and institutions. The sheltering coastal mountains and warm Pacific currents give it the mildest climate in the country. It can boast six hours of sunshine per day on average, and the flowers, which one sees everywhere, bloom all year around!

Victoria is a place for strollers and slow-paced sightseers and the Laurel Point Inn provides a decidedly pleasant base of operations.

S.S. Princess Marguerite *berths close to Laurel Point*

Routes and Distances

Laurel Point Inn is no more than a ten-minute walk from the Empress along the edge of Victoria Harbour, so follow directions in the Empress chapter to get to Laurel Point, either via the S.S. *Marguerite* from Seattle, the M.V. *Coho* from Port Angeles, or the British Columbia ferries from Tsawwassen.

Accommodations

We expected the rooms at Laurel Point to be fresh, clean, attractively furnished, and comfortable—and they are. Besides that, they are larger than most hotel rooms, with plenty of space for comfortable furniture in front of the windows, a great place for conversation.

In designing this hotel to make the most of the view, no two rooms could be exactly alike; the result is an interesting variety of angles and shapes. Each of the lower-floor rooms has a tiny balcony with a sliding door opening onto it. Some of the top, fourth-floor rooms have larger decks with outdoor furniture. Room rates vary according to the size of the room and how high it is in the hotel.

Before we first visited Laurel Point, friends who had occupied one of the fourth-floor rooms explained that enjoying the room itself was the best part of their trip to Victoria. The inn makes a point of leaving a daily paper outside every door, and our friends remember with particular pleasure a Sunday morning spent on their balcony in the sunshine: reading the paper, having a room-service breakfast with Bloody Marys, and watching the parade of ship and plane traffic on the water below.

In summertime the whole city, including the Laurel Point Inn, is apt to be booked up. There are cancellations, but a reservation a week or more in advance is usually necessary. If you come without one, the nearest available room may be thirty miles up island. Winters are a different story; then reservations at the inn are available on very short notice. This (plus no waiting to get into restaurants or places of interest) often makes winter the most pleasant time for this getaway vacation.

Victoria's Parliament buildings near Laurel Point

Activities

Laurel Point's on-premise activities tempt its guests to stay put and relax. Inside the V formed by the shape of the building is a wide terrace, with lounge furniture and umbrellas, where meals and beverages are served in good weather. One side of the V is flanked by an indoor swimming pool whose glass doors can be rolled back, converting it into part of the terrace. On the other side are tennis courts, positioned so loungers can observe the play. People who like hot tubs and Jacuzzis will enjoy the big, tiled hot spa next to the swimming pool. Victoria's excellent climate makes the terrace usable a large part of the year. When it is not, the sliding doors are shut to enclose the pool, and a plastic bubble is erected over one of the tennis courts, enabling you to play ball or swim during the winter months, too.

Despite the inn's obvious attractions, nobody should visit Victoria without spending some time seeing the sights. Read about Victoria's shopping and sight-seeing opportunities, for which the city is particularly famous, in "The Empress Hotel" chapter. In nice weather it is a pleasant walk around the end of the harbor, past the ship berths, to the heart of town where the shops and sights begin. If you do not want to walk to town, use the inn's free jitney service.

If you come here by automobile or boat, you will be rewarded if you bring bicycles. Many local residents use them routinely, so cyclists are a common sight on the streets, and motorists treat them courteously. There are places in Victoria that can best be seen by walking, and others so far out of town that a sight-seeing bus is preferable, but for covering everything in between at your own pace, nothing can beat a bicycle.

Should it prove impractical to bring your own, all kinds of rentals

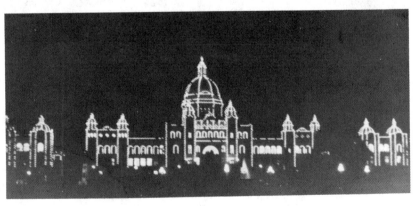

Parliament buildings at night

are available in town. Tandems are popular. Couples ride them everywhere, exploring side streets downtown and throughout the elegant older residential districts. After having seen the urban sights, a good ride from the inn is out along Dallas Road to Beacon Hill Park, which has a number of quiet trails and a five-mile stretch of rocky coastline hard upon the Strait of Juan de Fuca.

Dining

All food service at Laurel Point is in one general area. The coffee shop is separated from the dining room by a row of large sliding panels, which open to create one big room when needed. The furnishings of the two rooms are coordinated in design and color, but the tables and chairs in the coffee shop are less formal. The dining room is named The Wickers after the high-backed wicker chairs with which it is furnished.

The dinner menu has a variety of entrées balanced between meat and seafood, all consistently well prepared. Entrée prices are moderate, but salads, appetizers, and soups cost extra. Service is attentive and cheerful.

For a pleasant lunch with a nice view of the harbor, try Cook's Landing—the hotel's bright, airy cocktail lounge—popular at noontime. Fish and chips, generous, tasty salads, and oversized sandwiches are special attractions.

A decision to go out on the town for dinner presents only one problem—how to choose one spot when so many good ones are close by. You might begin with the Captain's Palace, just a block from the inn on Belleville Street. It specializes in seafood and is located in a beautifully restored Victorian mansion. Pablo's, also in a restored house, is across from the inn on Quebec Street. Its fare, mainly of Spanish character, nevertheless features Cordon Bleu, said to be the best in town.

French restaurants abound, as Gallic cuisine is much in demand in Victoria. Le Premier on Fort Street, Chez Pierre on Yates, and Coq au Vin in Bastion Square are among the most popular. Bastion Square is also the address of Maiko Gardens, which has good authentic Japanese food, and the Coach and Four, an Old-English restaurant specializing in roast beef, steak-and-kidney pie, and rack of lamb.

For formal hotel dining, the Empress and Oak Bay Beach hotels are outstanding, while the Parrot House, on top of the elegant Chateau Victoria Hotel, offers a panoramic view of the harbor from the only rooftop restaurant in town.

This is by no means a complete list, but it should convey the idea that Victoria is a city of restaurants as well as a city of gardens.

Central
Getaways

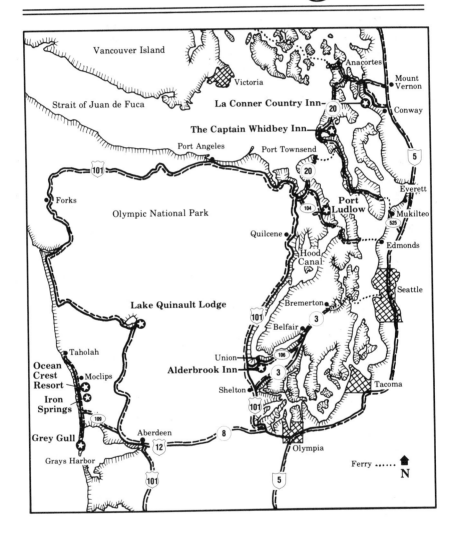

Vancouver Island

Anacortes

Mount Vernon

Victoria

Conway

La Conner Country Inn

Strait of Juan de Fuca

20

The Captain Whidbey Inn

Port Angeles

Port Townsend

20

5

Forks

Everett

Olympic National Park

104

Port Ludlow

Mukilteo

525

Quilcene

Hood Canal

Edmonds

Seattle

Lake Quinault Lodge

Bremerton

101

101

3

Belfair

Taholah

Union

106

Ocean Crest Resort

Moclips

Alderbrook Inn

3

Tacoma

Iron Springs

Shelton

109

101

Grey Gull

Aberdeen

8

Grays Harbor

12

Olympia

Ferry ......

101

5

N

La Conner Country Inn

Distances:

From Seattle—80 miles; allow 1½ hours

From Portland—260 miles; allow 6 hours

From Vancouver, B.C.—94 miles; allow 2 hours

Features:

Museums, restored buildings, waterfront activity, many shops and eating places; lush, quiet farming area

Activities:

Waterfront strolling, browsing, bicycling, marine tours, fishing, golf

Seasons:

Year-round; reservations for summer and fall should be made weeks in advance

Rates:

$43 to $47 for two people; Garden Cottage suite, $95

Address:

Second and Washington, La Conner, Washington 98257

Phone:

(206) 466-3101

The La Conner Country Inn and Restaurant

The La Conner Country Inn might well be the perfect example of an ideal getaway vacation spot. La Conner is a small, out-of-the-way community that has rebuilt itself in a way delightfully recapturing the times when logging, shipping, and fishing were the mainstays of life in the Northwest. In those days, before the automobile, everything here moved by water. Logs were floated to the mills, lumber was shipped out on the decks of square-rigged sailing ships and early steamers, machinery for the mills was delivered by boat, and the fishing industry was always bustling. The waterfront was the center of activity, and of course, the shops and taverns were also right there, intermingled with the docks.

The reconstructed town of La Conner is much as it was then, strung out along the east side of the Swinomish waterway, which still provides safe passage for vessels going up the sound in the lee of Whidbey Island. Rafts of logs still follow tow boats through the channel, and commercial fishermen tie up in front of the waterfront restaurants. Picturesque shops display antiques and memorabilia of the past. Good eating places, friendly taverns, and tearooms abound. Crafts and art work are everywhere.

A quick change of pace, a change of scene, and quiet comfort are the ingredients for a revitalizing experience, and this place has them all—and more.

Routes and Distances

Find La Conner by driving north from Seattle and Portland on Interstate 5, turning left a few miles before Mount Vernon at Conway, and then following the signs to La Conner.

From Vancouver take 99 and I-5 to Burlington. Turn west onto Washington 20 and proceed approximately ten miles, turning left twice at signs announcing La Conner and Shelter Harbor. Six miles after the second turn you will reach your destination.

Accommodations

Visitors have only one choice for a night's accommodation in La Conner; fortunately, the Country Inn is an excellent hostelry. It complements the town's turn-of-the-century motif, but it also has the advantages of new construction. It is centrally located, just a block from the waterfront, so that no point of interest is more than an easy stroll away.

The inn has twenty guest rooms and one large family suite. The rooms are big, airy, and comfortably furnished, each with a large brass bedstead, table and chairs, and a gas-burning fireplace. Bathrooms are spacious and comfortable. The suite has its own kitchen and wood-burning fireplace, and can take up to six people. In the morning you can enjoy a complimentary continental breakfast in one of the easy chairs around the large central fireplace in the "library."

Parking space for automobiles is close to the rooms, and there is even a bicycle shed. Guests are expected to carry their own luggage.

While reservations are advisable during the summer and fall, it is usually safe on winter weekdays just to call ahead in the morning and arrange rooms on a drop-in basis.

Activities

The main attractions in La Conner are the historic buildings and museums. You can see virtually everything—the yarn shops, galleries, pottery studios, antiques, food shops—by strolling from one end of town to the other, then up the small hill to City Hall and the one-hundred-year-old Gaches mansion. It is almost impossible to miss any of the highlights, but be sure to allow plenty of time to poke into everything and absorb the flavor of the town.

If you want a different perspective, put on a warm jacket and try a boat tour of the Swinomish Slough on the stern-wheeler *Harbor Queen*. It makes four hour-long trips a day.

Bicyclists are especially fond of La Conner as a starting place for expeditions over the Skagit flats—some of the most productive and beautiful farmland in the state. (The Northwest Bicycle Touring Society holds its one-hundred-mile bike race here every September.)

The country roads are flat and traffic is relatively sparse. Cyclists should take their own bikes; rentals cannot be counted on.

Sports fishermen can make arrangements for charter boats or rentals at the marina north of town. Golfers will find a good course about seven miles out along the road to Anacortes.

Deception Pass State Park on Whidbey Island is only fifteen miles to the west. Drive there with a picnic to enjoy the rugged scenery and watch the breathtaking rush of water through the pass at every change of the tide. For a more tranquil setting, spread your picnic on a grassy knoll overlooking the quiet waters of little Cranberry Lake in the interior of the park.

Dining

There are several good places to eat in La Conner. The inn's own restaurant offers a varied and attractive menu. It is open for lunch and dinner seven days a week, with champagne brunches on Saturdays and Sundays from 9 A.M. to 3 P.M. Its English pub lounge provides cocktail service.

The Black Swan, recently relocated on First Street, around the corner from the inn, offers imaginative, well-prepared dishes for

Town of La Conner from across Swinomish Channel

lunch and dinner seven days a week. Reservations are advisable.

The Lighthouse Inn is La Conner's largest and best-known eating place. It overlooks the waterway, and nearly every table has an excellent view of the marine traffic in the channel. Again, seafood is the house specialty, and can be counted on to be fresh and attractively prepared; prices are moderate. First-time guests will probably want a window table and will enjoy lingering over the meal. A wood-paneled cocktail lounge behind the dining area also has a view of the water traffic. Live music is provided on Thursday, Friday, and Saturday evenings.

The atmosphere in La Conner is informal, so jeans and sports clothes are all you need to be presentable in any of these eating places.

Among the shops along the main street are also half a dozen or more delis, tearooms, and taverns that serve luncheons and snacks. Most are owner-operated and quaintly decorated. They provide specialty foods that make them fun to try for breakfasts and midday meals.

The Captain Whidbey Inn

Distances:

From Seattle—61 miles, plus ferry; allow 2½ hours

From Portland—241 miles, plus ferry; allow 5½ hours

From Vancouver, B.C.—121 miles; allow 2¾ hours

Features:

Extremely quiet lodging; quaint, scenic

Activities:

Bicycling, hiking, beachcombing, exploring Coupeville, antique hunting, sailing, and rowing

Seasons:

Year-round; weekend reservations should be made well in advance

Rates:

$30 to $65 for two people

Address:

2072 W. Whidbey Island Inn Road, Coupeville, Washington 98239

Phone:

(206) 678-4097

The Captain Whidbey Inn built of madrona logs.

At The Captain Whidbey Inn on quiet and scenic Whidbey Island, the main activity is inactivity, for rest and relaxation are pure pleasure in this quaint old hostelry built of madrona logs in 1907. Perched on a low bluff overlooking the calm waters of Penn Cove, only a few miles from historic Coupeville, the inn stands just as it did when it was built so long ago. And that is how the owners want it to stay, for it is one of the few remaining old-style family inns, which are so rapidly becoming extinct in this country.

Arriving at night, you get your first pleasant feelings about this place, for all you can see in the dark woods, silhouetted against sky and water, is the large building with a lighted porch and an inviting glow in the four windows. Once you push open the heavy door, you can see that much of the friendly light comes from the huge fireplace in the communal room. Additional soft lighting comes from lanterns and candles, which enrich the interest of the antiques, paintings, and memorabilia that fill every nook and cranny. You quickly feel as if you have stepped back into the leisurely past, and at last there is time to read that neglected book or quietly stroll the beach without any particular destination. Actually, besides rest and relaxation there are many interesting things to do in the vicinity, but it may take some time to break the spell of the inn itself before you seek them out.

Routes and Distances

From Seattle proceed north on Interstate 5 to exit 189 just south of Everett, where a prominent sign marks the way to Washington 526 and the Mukilteo ferry. Take 526 west and be sure to look for the Boeing 747 manufacturing plant on the right. It is the largest clear-span building in the world. When 526 merges with 525, follow the latter to the ferry landing.

This ferry route is heavily traveled and two or three boats shuttle back and forth constantly between Mukilteo and the Columbia Beach landing on Whidbey. Call (206) 464-6400 in Seattle (toll free elsewhere in Washington—1-800-542-0810) for schedule and fare information. The actual ferry ride is twenty minutes, and departure times are less than thirty minutes apart, so waits are not long except during rush hour. On the Whidbey side there is a thirty-mile drive up the island. Proceed on Washington 525 to Coupeville, then take 20 for about three miles to the head of Penn Cove, where a sign directs you back along the waterfront to The Captain Whidbey. Portlanders take I-5 to Seattle, then follow the Seattle route to the inn.

Vancouverites take 99 and I-5 south to Burlington and turn right onto Washington 20. Go west on 20 and then follow it south across Deception Pass. Proceed through Oak Harbor to the head of Penn Cove, where there is a junction and a sign advising to go straight ahead to Coupeville. Instead, take a left turn onto the road that follows the beach. The Captain Whidbey Inn is one mile and to the left along this road.

Accommodations

The rooms on the second floor of the old inn building are the most popular even though the bathrooms are across the hall and the plank floors are uneven and creak when people move about. All the rooms have delightful views of the cove, are cozy, and are furnished with genuine antiques and comfortable beds. Two narrow stairways lead downstairs from the upper hall: one to the pub that adjoins the dining room, and one through the well-stocked mezzanine library to the communal room and lobby. Rates for the inn rooms are relatively low. If you plan to take one, remember the unattached baths and bring bathrobes.

The Lagoon Rooms, modern units with private bathrooms, are in new buildings fifty yards south of the old inn. The rooms are built of dark, natural wood with exposed beams and are named for the series of primitive tidal basins over which they look. In the morning you awake to the quacking of ducks and the cries of gulls, and looking out the window at the view, feel a million miles away from the hurly-burly of the city.

View from Lagoon Rooms at The Captain Whidbey Inn

The third rooming alternative is one of the "cottages"—really little cabins—scattered on the property overlooking Penn Cove. Each has a sitting room, bedroom, kitchenette, and fireplace. Pets are permitted here.

It is required to book a room for at least two nights on weekends, and three nights on holidays. Reservations should be made at least a month ahead for the summer season and important holidays, a week ahead for weekends in the winter, but you can often get weekday accommodations in the winter on short notice.

Activities

Many guests come to The Captain Whidbey Inn just to catch up on their reading. The library above the communal room is well stocked for pleasant browsing among hundreds of books. People take them downstairs to read in front of the fire in the winter, into the pub to read while they sip, or out onto the lawn overlooking the cove.

Joggers can run along the level road around the end of Penn Cove. Traffic is sparse, the clear salt air is invigorating, and the scenery makes distances seem short.

The level roads are also good for bicycling, and the inn rents English three-speed bikes to guests. Some people fly here from Seattle-Tacoma Airport via Harbor Airlines and use bicycles for all their local transportation. (Those who fly in will be picked up at the Oak Harbor airport without charge.) Serious bikers should bring their own bicycles; the inn has only one ten-speed for rent.

Try to schedule at least half a day for browsing around the old Victorian section of Coupeville. By either bicycle or auto it is only a short time away. Park the vehicle, stroll about, and perhaps have lunch. There are crafts shops and a museum to see, and a blockhouse built by settlers during the Indian uprisings. Coupeville is also an antique lover's paradise. Shops invite browsers, and here on out-of-the-way Whidbey Island are some of the most complete and authentic inventories in the Northwest.

Across the island, only two miles from the inn, are Point Partridge and Fort Ebey State Park, from which miles and miles of unspoiled agate and driftwood beaches extend southward toward Admiralty Head. Around Admiralty Head is the Keystone Underwater State Park. Scuba divers use it year-round and make The Captain

Fireplace wall in pub of The Captain Whidbey Inn

Whidbey Inn their headquarters. (A dive shop in Oak Harbor supplies air and equipment.)

Hikers will enjoy not only the beaches, but also the trails in Fort Ebey State Park, where a pretty little lake makes a pleasant destination. You also can hike around Crockett's Lake at Fort Casey State Park, farther down the coast, where another authentic blockhouse can be examined.

Because of the mild weather, golf at the Oak Harbor public course, about nine miles from the inn, is a year-round activity. The park at Coupeville has a public tennis court. The golf course is adequate. The tennis court is of marginal quality.

The inn maintains a small dock for the convenience of visiting boaters, and there are a half-dozen aluminum rowboats for rent to fishermen, exercisers, and explorers.

Dining

The Captain Whidbey dining room is the only eating area at the inn, but it is open for three meals a day, year-round. It is a charming room with paneled walls and ceiling and madrona beams and posts. Windows running along one side provide a magnificent view of Penn Cove. To add to the cozy atmosphere, there is a huge fireplace, and in chilly weather there is always a fire.

Breakfast and lunch at the inn are excellent and reasonably priced. The dinner menu is limited to six or seven entrées, but all can be counted on to be very good.

No matter how satisfactory the food, it is often nice to get away for a change and the old section of Coupeville just a few miles down the road affords several interesting opportunities. One is the Knead and Feed, a tiny restaurant and bakery overlooking the water. It serves delicious lunches of homemade soup and sandwiches that are made with bread fresh from the oven. An even smaller place—just five tables—that also serves good soups and sandwiches (plus beer and wine) is Michael's Your Place, farther down the street.

Coupeville also has a Chinese restaurant, The Six Persimmons, which serves excellent food, but unfortunately is open only for lunch.

The Admiralty Resort at Port Ludlow

Distances:
From Seattle—32 miles, plus ferry; allow 1¼ hours
From Portland—215 miles, plus ferry; allow 4 hours
From Vancouver, B.C.—151 miles, plus ferry; allow 3¾ hours

Features:
Heavily forested natural setting on the water; the closest of the getaways to Seattle; meticulous, well-planned development

Activities:
Saltwater sports, beach activities, golf, tennis, walking, bicycling, squash, swimming

Seasons:
Year-round; summer season usually requires reservations several weeks in advance

Rates:
$55 to $94 for two people in summer; $38 to $76 in winter

Address:
Route 1, Box 75, Port Ludlow, Washington 98365

Phone:
(206) 437-2222; toll free in Seattle, 622-9020; elsewhere in Washington, 1-800-732-1239

The Admiralty at Port Ludlow

Port Ludlow was once a roaring mill town and lumber port. Now the town is gone, and only a few crumbled concrete foundations indicate the old mill site. In place of the town, the Pope and Talbot company—which used to run the mill—has spent years carefully reforesting the area and developing a residential-resort complex that takes advantage of the splendid natural setting.

At the head of the harbor, above a marina, is the focal point of the resort—the Admiralty—where you will find the front desk, restaurant, and lounge. A large lawn area, big enough for landing light planes, stretches from the Admiralty to the beach. Around a bend in the road is the "beach club" with its swimming pool and squash and tennis courts, and beyond the club lie guest accommodations and condominium units. All the buildings are low and display the muted grays and browns of natural wood.

Back from the waterfront everything is heavily forested. Trails through the trees offer endless fine views of the harbor and sound, both always bustling with boating activity, and the jagged Olympic mountain range. From the high ground of the golf course, the scenery is magnificent enough to endanger any player's concentration.

Routes and Distances
During a storm in early 1979 the Hood Canal floating bridge, which put Port Ludlow a little over an hour away from Seattle, broke

away from its moorings and sank. Reconstruction is underway, and the new bridge is scheduled to be in operation in the fall of 1982 or early 1983. Meanwhile, the state ferry system has put ferries into service between Lofall and South Point to reconnect the Olympic Peninsula with the mainland.

The most direct route to Port Ludlow from Seattle begins with the Winslow ferry to Bainbridge Island. Cross Bainbridge and the Agate Pass Bridge on Washington 305 until it merges with Washington 3. Take 3 north either to Lofall and the ferry, or to the Hood Canal Bridge, once it is completed. Either alternative puts you onto Washington 104, which you follow for less than four miles to the marked side road to the right leading to Port Ludlow.

Portland getaways are unaffected by the bridge troubles. Take Interstate 5 to Olympia and change to U.S. 101. Go through Shelton and Quilcene. Ten miles past Quilcene, turn east onto Washington 104 and continue driving (about ten miles) to the Port Ludlow turnoff. After a left turn it is five miles to the resort.

From Vancouver, drive to Burlington and take Route 20 across the Deception Pass Bridge to Whidbey Island. Stay on 20 to the Keystone ferry landing. Take the short ferry ride across to Port Townsend and from there continue on Route 20 for five more miles, then take the cutoff to Chimacum and Hadlock. From there follow the signs to Mats Mats and Port Ludlow.

Port Ludlow condominiums bordering tennis courts

Accommodations

All the rental units are in small buildings scattered between one and two hundred yards from the Admiralty building and the beach club. Each building contains two, three, or four units. Accommodations range from a single bedroom with bath to a suite with kitchen, living room, fireplace, deck, and up to four bedrooms. Each bedroom contains two twin beds or a queen-size bed. (State a preference when making reservations.) The rooms are generally bright and cheerful with comfortable, contemporary furnishings. All the units are angled to ensure nice views, as well as privacy.

For summer weekends, reservation lead time is several weeks; in the winter it varies. Midweek reservations can often be obtained on the spur of the moment.

Activities

Port Ludlow offers a variety of things to do, ranging from the strenuous to the sedentary. The moderate climate makes it possible to engage in many of the outdoor sports year-round; the foremost of these—without question—is golf. Ever since this resort was built, it has been noted for the excellence of its eighteen-hole championship course, which combines treacherous lies with exceptional scenic beauty. (Guests at the resort pay a greens fee.)

Tennis can be played most months of the year, barring rain. The courts have Laykold-type surfaces and are in excellent condition. There is no charge for guests but reservations are necessary. Four of the seven courts are booked with the attendant in the beach club office, while the other three, located adjacent to the golf course, are reserved through the well-equipped pro shop. Tennis balls and shoes can be obtained here, too, but the shop is a long way from most of the tennis courts, and tennis-playing guests may want to bring their own gear.

For squash players there is a regulation court in the lower level of the beach club. The club also contains a large, beautiful swimming pool with a diving board. It is not covered, so the swimming season lasts only from May until early October. At that time the pool is closed, but clear waters and fascinating marine life are always waiting for hardy scuba divers.

Boating is a major activity at Port Ludlow. It is pleasant to sit and watch the boats coming and going at the marina, but you also can rent a sailboat or motorboat and join the parade. Boats can be rented for trolling, but fishermen should bring their own tackle. There is excellent fishing for steelhead, salmon, and trout, and the beaches in the area yield oysters and clams. At low tide, it is enjoyable to walk the beaches looking for interesting rocks and driftwood.

Golfers at Port Ludlow enjoy spectacular views

Several paved bicycle paths have been built around the Admiralty complex. There are also many miles of quiet and scenic residential roads throughout the development that are adapted to cycling and from which you can observe much interesting architecture. Bicycles can be rented in the summertime.

For those who would rather hike, the old logging roads cut through the woods years ago make good hiking trails.

There are more activities in the summer months, but golf, hiking, and fishing are popular whenever the weather permits, right through the winter. And many people come in the off-season just to relax. They bring their own reading material and other incidentals, although a small "Grocerie and Gen'l Store" can be found about a mile down the road to Mats Mats.

The beach club building is the center for indoor activities. There is a game room with table tennis and pool tables on the lower level, and tables are set up for bridge in the lounge upstairs, making it a cheery retreat on a rainy day.

In the Wreck Room Lounge you can dance to live music every evening from May through September. In the winter months a combo plays on Friday and Saturday nights; at other times a big nickelodeon provides the music.

Dining

The Harbormaster dining room fills the whole upper level of the resort's main building. It is a long, narrow room decorated with timber pilings and anchor chains to create a nautical flavor. Tables are grouped near large windows, which provide fine views of the harbor activity. The dinner menu is excellent, balanced between seafood and meat dishes. A good wine list is available and prices are moderate except for the lobster, which is expensive. The Harbormaster also serves breakfast and lunch year-round.

Casual clothing is generally in order at Port Ludlow, but most guests like to dress a little more formally at dinner. Neckties are not required anywhere in the area, but many men wear them, and most wear jackets in cool weather and sports shirts and slacks in the summer. Women dress with equal formality.

In the spring and summer months a small delicatessen on the lower floor has tables both inside and outdoors on the lawn. It serves novel sandwiches and seems to be a favorite of boaters coming into the marina as well as of resort guests and local residents.

For variety, you can try the new Timber House restaurant in Quilcene. It is a leisurely twenty-five-minute drive from Port Ludlow to this little peninsula town. When visitors see more cars parked in the Timber House lot than in all the rest of the town, they rightly suspect that the trip has been worthwhile.

Quilcene is famous for its oysters and the Timber House has a fine seafood menu, featuring a number of outstanding oyster dishes. The charcoal-broiled steaks are of equal quality, and all meals are served in elegant "big city" style. Prices here are moderate.

A different but, in its way, equally rewarding place to eat is the Ajax Cafe in Hadlock. Another twenty-five-minute drive from Port Ludlow, the Ajax might best be described as funky and fun. Located right on the shore of Puget Sound in an ancient, white clapboard building with checked window panes and remarkable decoration, it is the spirit of informality. Its nine tables are covered with oil cloth and have fresh flowers and candles. The menu ranges from steaks to spaghetti and hot sandwiches, and prices are modest. Beer and wine are served, but not hard liquor.

Ocean Crest Resort

Distances:
From Seattle—140 miles; allow 2¾ hours
From Portland—184 miles; allow 3¾ hours

Features:
Secluded oceanfront resort on a high bluff; magnificent views, and some of the finest dining on the Washington coast

Activities:
Clam digging, beachcombing, use of heated indoor pool and whirlpool spa, winter storm watching

Seasons:
Year-round; two-night minimum stay required on weekends and three-night minimum on holidays and minus tides

Rates:
$26 to $58 per night for two people; suites available from $50 to $60 for two

Address:
Moclips, Washington 98562

Phone:
(206) 276-4465

The Ocean Crest Resort perches on a cliffside

An interesting phenomenon about beach resorts is that they need little besides the ocean and beach to entertain their guests. In the main, people who enjoy going to the seaside are content to take long strolls along the wet sand, always keeping a sharp eye out for a shiny agate or an interesting piece of driftwood, or to prop themselves up against a log and watch the surf break endlessly against the shore.

The broad, sandy beach at the Ocean Crest Resort meets the standards of even the most discriminating beachcomber and, in addition, is one of the finest spots on the coast to dig for the elusive razor clam. True, the resort is on a high bluff which necessitates a bit of a trail walk to reach the beach, but the spectacular view from above more than compensates for the short hike down to water level. Also, since swimming is somewhat limited in the cold waters of the Washington coast, the indoor pool and hot spa at Ocean Crest are a bonus for those who vacation here.

But the real distinguishing feature of the Ocean Crest Resort is the first-class restaurant on the premises. Though many of the units have kitchens, few guests pass up the opportunity to have at least some of their meals in this delightful restaurant, reputedly one of the finest on the coast. Beachcombers will be happy to know that they don't have to dress up just because the food is elegant; casual attire is the rule here, as it is everywhere along this stretch of coast.

Routes and Distances

The Ocean Crest Resort is located on the seaward side of Highway 109, just south of Moclips and eight miles from where the highway terminates at the Taholah Indian Reservation. To get to the resort, drive to Aberdeen and Hoquiam and pick up Highway 109, which runs west to the coast. After it turns north at the coast, continue for thirteen miles to the resort.

Accommodations

Although the prices at Ocean Crest vary widely, most of the rooms fall near the middle of the range. The low end of the scale covers what the resort refers to as "Sleeping Rooms." These are small hotel-type rooms with no view, but for the economy-minded who plan to spend most of their time on the beach or elsewhere, they are more than adequate. Each comes with a double bed and basic furniture, a color television, and a coffeemaker.

At the other end of the price scale is the "Honeymoon Suite," a very large room with a king bed and a balcony offering a spectacular ocean view. It has a dressing area with a sink and vanity, as well as another sink in the bath and a cozy corner fireplace and a refrigerator.

In between these extremes are most of the standard rooms, all large and much alike, with individual balconies and queen beds. Pricing variations in this group are determined by the degree of view and whether or not the rooms have fireplaces or refrigerators.

There are also some one-bedroom suites that are quite reasonably priced. These units have either a full kitchen or an efficiency kitchen (two burners, refrigerator and sink, but no oven), and the living rooms have studio couches so that the suite can sleep four people comfortably. The base price for these suites is for two people: each additional person is charged $6 extra.

Finally, for even larger groups, there are two two-bedroom apartments, one with a view and one without, priced accordingly.

Ocean Crest offers a midweek getaway package during the off-season (October 1 through March 1) when guests can stay three nights for the price of two. It is a perfect time to do a little beachcombing, or if you happen to be lucky enough to time your visit right, some winter storm watching.

Activities

The seasonal activities pattern at Ocean Crest goes like this: spring and fall, dig clams; summer, laze on the beach; winter, beachcomb, watch storms, and go steelheading.

Clamming, of course, is a low-tides activity. Seasoned clammers

Working the low tide for razor clams

know their tide tables and plan well ahead, especially in making reservations for the minus-tide periods. If possible, they like to take a kitchenette unit so they can eat their early catch at the resort and then take the last day's clams home while they are still fresh. The resort has an outdoor sink and counter at the top of the beach stairway for the convenience of clam cleaners. It gets a lot of use because this long, wide stretch of beach is a magnificent producer that turns few diggers away without a good catch.

Lazing in the summer needs no elaboration. Take magazines, suntan lotion, and a picnic lunch and make a day of it. If you don't want to hike down the stairway that leads through a forested glen to the ocean, drive south or north a half-mile or so to access roads that allow you to take your car onto the beach. The sand here is as solid and level as an asphalt highway, and you can drive for miles to find just the right place to stop.

In the winter, the most fun is to bundle up and walk the beach, looking for Japanese glass floats and other castaways, and then go back to your room, light a cheery fire in the fireplace, and watch the ever-changing weather outside from your snug sanctuary. Or you might first use the heated pool and the hot spa to remove any residual chill and then settle down by the fire.

There are three good steelheading rivers not too far from the resort. The Quinault, only eight miles to the north at Taholah, is the closest. You can fish from the bank on any of these streams, but that is difficult for strangers unfamiliar with the territory. The best way to try for these fighting fish is to hire a guide, which can be arranged by the management of the inn on your behalf. The local guides are mostly native Indians, Quinaults, who know the rivers and the fish and supply a boat and any necessary tackle. Native guides are almost mandatory for fishing the Quinault, in fact, because it is on the reservation, and a guided trip is an interesting experience. The boats are genuine dugouts and the guides will take you to places where there are seldom other fishermen, and where you can absorb the character of the rain forest rivers as they have been since long before civilization encroached on the Olympic Peninsula.

The winter steelheading season starts around the first of November every year and lasts until spring. For year-round sport, surf casting for sea perch is always popular. These little fish yield beautiful white fillets and can be taken almost any time right in front of Ocean Crest Resort.

Dining

Ocean Crest is unique among Washington's seaside resorts in that it has its own first-class Dinner House Restaurant which serves not only its own guests, but people from all the other resorts along this stretch of coast.

Jess and Barbara Curtright established the Dinner House many

Many come just to dine at the Dinner House

years ago and built a reputation for excellence that is being zealously maintained by the new generation of Curtrights carrying on the old traditions.

The menu emphasizes seafood, but also includes good veal and chicken dishes, as well as steaks and chops. No dishes are prepared ahead of time; guests are served chowder made with razor clams from the beach and crisp green salads while the entrée is being cooked. The dining room is situated on the very edge of the high bluff, looking out over the ocean. At night a powerful floodlight illuminates the surf, and although the desserts after dinner are homemade and difficult to resist, it is also pleasant to order a cappuccino and linger a while to enjoy the dramatic view.

Every room has its own coffeemaker and guests must rely on that for sustenance until 10:00 A.M., when the restaurant opens for brunch. Omelets and sandwiches are available until 2:00 P.M.

For dining variety you can go into Ocean Shores, about a twenty-minute drive. The newest place there, which is already gaining a well-deserved reputation for fine cuisine, is the Onion Patch. It is a small, intimate restaurant with a good wine list and an excellent menu that changes frequently, with daily specials posted on a blackboard near the entrance. The table coverings are ordinary white butcher paper—crayons are furnished so that guests can decorate their own place settings.

Alderbrook Inn

Distances:
From Seattle—26 miles, plus ferry; allow 1¾ hours
From Portland—154 miles; allow 3¼ hours
From Vancouver, B.C.—173 miles, plus ferry; allow 5½ hours

Features:
Quiet beach resort, seems very remote but is actually close to Seattle

Activities:
Golf, beach walking, tennis, fishing, swimming, oyster picking

Seasons:
Year-round

Rates:
$53 to $58 for two people in lanai and plaza rooms; cottages $75 to $90; suites $75

Address:
Union, Washington 98592

Phone:
(206) 898-2200; toll free from Seattle, 622-2404 or 621-1119; toll free from Portland, 226-4202

The Alderbrook Inn on Hood Canal

Alderbrook is an old inn that has been modernized and recently expanded. The inn occupies 435 wooded acres on the lower end of Hood Canal, and is one of the few places in all of the Puget Sound area where the salt water is warm enough—at least in the summer—for enjoyable swimming. The weather here at the "hook" of the canal is generally nice from spring through fall, the Olympic Mountains rise grandly to the west, and oysters and clams abound. In short, though the lower canal is less than a two-hour drive from Seattle, it seems light-years away.

Despite the attractions of its serene setting, Alderbrook is often not fully booked in the late fall and winter, and a quick telephone call then can often obtain a reservation on the spur of the moment.

Tennis and outdoor swimming generally are not possible in the off-season, but weather is often good enough for all of the other activities. Even if fog and rain should set in, view it as a happy excuse to hole up with a good book, rest, eat, enjoy the indoor pool, and loaf for a few days before returning to the workaday world.

Routes and Distances

From Seattle take the Bremerton ferry. There are eighteen sailings a day. Ride fifty-five minutes and then drive south on

Washington 3, following the signs to Belfair. Just out of Bremerton is an excellent view of the historic battleship *Missouri*, tied up alongside three moth-balled World War II aircraft carriers. A short distance past Belfair, Hood Canal can be seen on the right. Take Washington 106 from here for thirteen miles to the inn.

One alternate route from the Seattle area is the Fauntleroy ferry to Southworth, then 160 to Gorst to join Washington 3. Another is a drive south on Interstate 5 to Olympia and then north on U.S. 101 for twenty-eight miles to Washington 106. A right onto 106 and then nine miles will bring you to the inn. From Tacoma the Narrows Bridge provides the most direct access to Hood Canal.

Portlanders take I-5 to Olympia and follow the Seattle alternate route north along 101 and 106.

From Vancouver the quickest trip is to drive 99 and I-5 to the Seattle ferry dock and then to follow the Seattle directions. An alternate route that avoids Seattle's traffic is to turn off I-5 at Edmonds and take a ferry ride to Kingston on the Olympic Peninsula. From here take the road to Poulsbo until it intersects Washington 3. Then follow 3 through Bremerton to Belfair and 106 from Belfair to the inn.

Mariners who come by boat will find a long dock extending from the main lodge with space for about twenty-five vessels. Moorage is free for guests of the inn.

Accommodations

The main building of the Alderbrook complex is brand new. It houses eating areas, meeting rooms, the lobby, and a bar. It also contains forty-seven "plaza" guest rooms, so named because they are arranged around three sides of an open court filled with planters of small trees. Each of these rooms has a private deck, and most have views of the canal and the mountains beyond. The rooms are not especially large, but there is space for a table and chairs, where one can read or write or have drinks while looking out over the scenery. Everything is clean and new.

Adjacent to the new building are thirty-six "lanai" rooms in a separate but still relatively modern building. These rooms are as well kept and comfortable as the plaza rooms, and have individual decks, but possibly not quite such good views.

The original Alderbrook Inn, built years ago, consisted of twenty-one housekeeping cottages arranged in a horseshoe pattern around a lawn facing the canal. These cottages remain, but have now been remodeled. Each has two bedrooms, a living room with fireplace, a kitchen, and a porch. Each accommodates four people comfortably and is suitable for a family or for two couples.

Reservations for summertime and holidays must be made sev-

Dock on Hood Canal welcomes boaters

eral weeks ahead. For weekdays and the off-season, only a short notice is necessary.

Activities

Alderbrook Inn tries to have something available for every taste. Golf, however, is the main outdoor attraction at Alderbrook. The golf course lies one and a half miles east of the inn on a high ridge overlooking the canal. When the sun shines it hits here early and quickly burns off the moisture common at lower elevations. The course, set among towering firs, is considered one of the finest in the state. A pro shop and snack bar are located on the first tee, and electric and pull carts can be rented.

A short drive from the pro shop are four well-maintained, hard-surfaced tennis courts. Tennis players must check in at the pro shop to reserve courts and to obtain tokens to open the court gates.

Next to the tennis courts is a small park area with covered picnic tables, barbecues, and a playground with swings and slides—handy for tennis-playing parents with children.

Few people visit Alderbrook without at least thinking about doing a little oyster picking. Shells litter the beaches, and when the tide is low, fat live oysters can be searched out and gathered. Be sure you have a container for them; each guest of the inn may pick eighteen oysters a day. Because young oyster larvae grow only on the old shells, *you must shuck your oysters on the beach and return the shells to the tide flats.* Underneath the oysters, buried in the gravel, are butter clams.

It is fun to walk the beaches at low tide and to stroll along the shoulder of the highway observing the homes perched ingeniously on narrow shelves and bits of land between the road and water. Bicycling is not good; shoulders are narrow and traffic is fast on the waterfront highway. Serious hikers can take trails through the woods and up the ridge to the east. Ask the inn management about finding the starts of these trails.

In the fall, those who know how to recognize them can have a fantastic time hunting mushrooms. The succulent chanterelle grows prolifically in the particular mini-clime around the south end of the canal. Hunters have been known to take home large finds of this delicacy from an afternoon's outing!

Whatever one does during the day, there is a covered, heated pool on the inn premises for an evening dip and a large, double Jacuzzi bath where one can relax, soothe tired muscles, and meet other guests in an informal atmosphere.

Dining

Breakfast, lunch, and dinner are served in the large Beachside Room. Cedar paneling, massive satin-finished cedar tables, and comfortable captain's chairs give the room its distinctive character. One entire side looks out over the canal, and many window tables are available. The food is attractively prepared, and the help is extremely friendly.

A veranda fronting the water side of the bar has a row of tables that make a pleasant place for outdoor cocktails in good weather.

A few hundred yards down the road and within easy walking distance is the quaint Robin Hood Inn. It specializes in seafood and steak combinations for dinner, three-egg omelettes with baby shrimp and bacon for breakfast. Prices are moderate, and there is a good wine list.

Lake Quinault Lodge

Distances:

From Seattle—160 miles; allow 3½ hours

From Portland—187 miles; allow 4 hours

From Vancouver, B.C.—301 miles; allow 7 hours

Features:

Quiet lake, majestic rain forest, seclusion

Activities:

Forest and ocean hiking, clamming, fishing, boating, swimming, game room activities

Seasons:

Year-round; summers and holidays are always busy, so last-minute reservations are easier to get from November through February

Rates:

$43 to $60 for two people

Address:

P.O. Box 7, Quinault, Washington 98575

Phone:

(206) 288-2571; or toll free from Washington 1-800-562-6672

The old main lodge at Lake Quinault

Lake Quinault Lodge may be the only place you ever go and hope it rains. Located in Washington's unmatchable rain forest, the lodge affords memorable experiences even when the weather is bad. In July and August you may have sunshine and warm days; other times prepare for rain, but seldom extreme cold. Take rain gear (three or four inches of rain in a day are not unusual) and plan to walk the ocean beaches and easy forest trails in order to assimilate a full measure of the area's grandeur.

There are no televisions or radios here. The management stresses a quiet, rustic atmosphere. The lodge's main building was constructed on the shore of the lake fifty years ago, and reflects the standards of comfort and elegance of the 1920s. In the spacious main lobby a massive fireplace, fed with three-foot logs, is surrounded by game tables and deep wicker chairs. The lobby is usually filled with bridge players, readers, and conversation groups.

This inn also offers excellent food, and is a near-perfect hideaway for those who just want to stretch out with a good book and let the world go by for a few days.

Routes and Distances
The shortest route for Seattle travelers is south through Tacoma and Olympia on Interstate 5, then west on Washington 8 to Elma, where you pick up U.S. 12 to Hoquiam, and finally north on U.S. 101

to the two-mile cutoff at the south shore of Lake Quinault.

Portlanders drive north on I-5 to Centralia and then on U.S. 12 to Elma, where they pick up the Seattle route. If time is available for a more scenic drive, take U.S. 30 up the Columbia through Saint Helens to Astoria. There cross the bridge to 101 and head north to Quinault.

From Vancouver it is a long drive to Lake Quinault through Seattle, Olympia, Aberdeen, and up the peninsula on U.S. 101 to the lake. A more relaxing way to go with less driving is to take the Tsawwassen ferry to Victoria and the *Coho* across the straits to Port Angeles. From there it is only 121 miles of driving. The total time elapsed will be as great, but the trip considerably more enjoyable.

Accommodations

The guest rooms in the main lodge retain the same period atmosphere as the lobby, although they have been modernized. Nevertheless, we recommend the "fireplace units" in the new wing. Each of these has a spacious sitting area furnished with a sofa, bridge table, and captain's chairs, and a private deck facing the lake. The fireplace burns gas logs—not quite so cozy as a wood-burning fireplace, perhaps, but the gas lights instantly, and any fireplace is cheerful to come back to after an outing in the rain. The beds are queen-size and comfortable.

Weekends must be booked on a two-night basis (Friday and Saturday), and three-day holidays must be booked for three nights. Most weekends and all three-day holidays are booked well in advance. Thanksgiving is the busiest period, often sold out a year ahead. Throughout the fall and winter, rooms are usually available during the week, but do call or write in advance if you want a fireplace unit, because they are the first to be taken. Do not hesitate to call on the spur of the moment; sometimes there are cancellations.

Activities

Well-marked trails near the lodge take you through stands of ancient, moss-covered cedar, fir, and hemlock. Nowhere can the grandeur of the rain forests be better appreciated. You may be able to see and photograph elk in the early morning or late evening when the animals come down for water.

The thirty-mile drive through the rain forest and around Lake Quinault is an experience not to miss. Allow a couple of hours for this drive; if possible, take a picnic to eat at Graves Creek Campground. On the way back stop at the bonsai nursery on the opposite side of the lake. It has an exceptionally interesting collection of plants, and visitors are welcomed.

In summer the Graves Creek Campground is the takeoff point for hikes into the Enchanted Valley, one of America's most remarkable hiking grounds. The valley trail leads directly across the very center of the Olympic Peninsula past mountains, glaciers, waterfalls, and a

Rain forest on a misty day behind Lake Quinault Lodge

wide range of forest environments.

Lake Quinault offers swimming, boating, and trout fishing during the summer. Steelheading is good in the upper Quinault River during the fall and winter.

The ocean beaches at Kalaloch, part of the Olympic National Park, are an easy forty-minute drive from the lodge. These are long, wide beaches on which automobiles are not allowed. They are particularly exciting during winter storms, when beachcombers like to look for Japanese glass floats and other drifting treasures. In summer the beaches invite sunning and picnicking. Swimming should be undertaken with caution because severe undertows are common.

The lodge itself provides a heated indoor swimming pool, a therapy pool, a sauna, and a game room equipped with table tennis, pool tables, and pinball machines, all of which may be useful for keeping children entertained. The big lawn has badminton nets and horseshoe pits. There is also an interesting and well-stocked gift shop.

The Forest Room opens for cocktails at five in the afternoon. In contrast to the general tranquility, the Forest Room can swing in the evening because it is the gathering place of young people employed at the Forest Service headquarters a short distance down the road.

Dining

There are no acceptable restaurants in the vicinity except for the lodge itself, but luckily, that is no hardship: lodge food is delightful and reasonably priced.

The dining room overlooks a wide lawn and the lake. Rustic, softly lighted, and decorated with a fifty-year collection of local artifacts, it is open all day. Casual clothing is in order, but some guests dress for dinner.

The menu offers a good selection of seafood and meat entrées, some of which are excellent. The wine list is ample for most tastes, and a good house wine is available by the carafe. Meals are served by young help in a relaxed and friendly manner.

The Grey Gull

Distances:

From Seattle—132 miles; allow 2½ hours

From Portland—165 miles; allow 3½ hours

From Vancouver, B.C.—277 miles; allow 5½ hours

Features:

Beach resort on the ocean; elegant condominium accommodations

Activities:

Beach activities, clamming, golf, bicycling, surf and charter fishing, bird watching

Seasons:

Open year-round; two-day minimum stay required weekends and holidays

Rates:

$45 to $72 for two people; $95 for large two-bedroom unit

Address:

P.O. Box 1417, Ocean Shores, Washington 98569

Phone:

(206) 289-3381

The Grey Gull from Ocean Shores beach

As alike as northwest beaches are in certain respects, each one differs markedly from the others in its shoreward environment and scenery and facilities, so each is a joy to discover individually and then rediscover again in different seasons. The Grey Gull is a condominium resort located on one of these special beaches—a huge, flat spit of sand, seven and a half miles long, between the Pacific Ocean and Gray's Harbor. Known as Ocean Shores, the spit is the site of one of the more grandiose development schemes ever to hit the Northwest. Ocean Shores is now incorporated into a town, with an area set aside in the middle of the spit for commercial activities: stores, the golf course, an airport, and a row of condominiums including the Grey Gull. The rest of the big spit is covered by a network of roads and canals (twenty-four miles of the latter alone) and is subdivided into thousands of sandy, bunch-grassed building lots. The unlikely locations and imaginative architecture of the houses that have been erected on these lots are often startling to the visitor cruising the area for the first time. Speculating on the life-style and intentions of those who have built here was one of our more fascinating activities at Ocean Shores.

But with all the interest the development generates, the orientation of the Grey Gull is always primarily to the beach. It occupies a desirable spot right at the broadest part and to guests who come to the Gull, that is often all they want. Everything else they can take or leave alone according to their mood; the beach offers occupation enough.

Routes and Distances

From Seattle and Vancouver, this trip is an easy drive on good roads all the way. Vancouverites take 99 and Interstate 5 to Seattle. From Seattle take I-5 south to Olympia and turn west at exit 104 onto Route 8, which merges later into Route 12. Follow the well-marked road through Aberdeen to Hoquiam. Here pick up Washington 109 and continue west until it reaches the coast. Then take a left turn and go south four miles to Ocean Shores and the Grey Gull.

Portlanders can drive to Ocean Shores one of two ways. Either go north on I-5 to Olympia and join the Seattle route, or turn off I-5 at Kelso and take the longer but more scenic route along the Columbia and Willapa Bay. For the latter, follow Washington 4 west from Kelso to its junction with U.S. 101 just south of Willapa Bay. Then follow 101 to Hoquiam and pick up the Seattle route.

For pilots a lighted airstrip, twenty-five hundred feet long and

Deep sea charters leave daily from Ocean Shores

suitable for private planes, lies directly behind the post office and barely a stone's throw from the condominiums. Fuel, light maintenance, and free tie-down facilities are available. There are no landing fees.

Accommodations

The Grey Gull's thirty-eight condominium units are particularly well designed and well kept up. Each has a balcony with an unobstructed view of the ocean, a wood-burning fireplace, a fully equipped kitchen, and a color television. A wood room in each wing of the building is kept well stocked with kindling and split logs. Your dog may go with you to fetch the wood, but he or she must be leashed.

The apartments have four basic designs. For a single couple the efficiency unit is a good value. It has a sitting area around the fireplace, a king-size bed, and a somewhat abbreviated kitchen in one large, airy room.

The one-bedroom suite is more commodious. It has a bedroom with a king-size bed, a fully equipped kitchen, and a sizable living-dining area. It is especially comfortable for a couple, but it can take four people if the sofa is converted to a double bed. A deluxe one-bedroom suite has a slightly larger living area and two double beds in the bedroom.

The largest unit, with two separate bedrooms and two baths, is quite comfortable for two couples to share and can accommodate a third couple on the sofa that makes into a double bed.

Summers are regularly booked ahead, but winter reservations are easy to get.

Activities

The Japan Current brings flotsam from all around the Pacific rim to the beaches of the Northwest. This makes beach walking, especially after a big blow, always an interesting experience. Who knows what new treasures tomorrow's tide may carry?

Next in popularity is clam digging at low tide. (Be sure to check at the resort about the newest clamming regulations.) This is a sport requiring skill and speed; it is not just a tedious excavation. The wily razor clam is the only shellfish capable of fleeing in self defense. It has a thin streamlined shell and a powerful digging foot enabling it to submerge rapidly in the soft wet sand. *Diggers are cautioned to help prevent the waste of clams by learning to dig carefully (allowing a minimum of breakage) and by keeping every clam that is dug.* Experience will teach you how to select the sign of larger clams. Since a two-year-old clam is three times larger than a yearling, it pays to be selective.

Jetty at Ocean Shores' Point Brown

There is contention among the natives as to which of the local beaches are the best clam producers, but this is without question one of the better ones. The season is open most of the year at Ocean Shores; it is closed only two months in the summer in order for the clam population to reproduce. To help its guests claim their share, the

Gull keeps extra clam shovels for rent and maintains a special clam cleaning room on the first floor of the north wing.

Surf casting for perch is another favorite pastime. Bait is sold locally, and all necessary gear can be rented. No license is needed.

The big marina at the south end of the spit sends out charter boats daily during the salmon and tuna seasons. A little restaurant at the marina starts serving buffet breakfasts at five in the morning, and the fishermen pile onto their boats from there, still munching and carrying their coffee.

Just to the southwest is Point Brown and the north Gray's Harbor jetty, which is a good spot for sighting such sea birds as kittiwakes, shearwaters, and murres. With a little luck, you may also observe harbor seals near the outer jetty or sight the offshore spouting of a gray whale.

If you bring a bike, you can ride it to Point Brown—and elsewhere—because the roads are flat and have little traffic.

Inland, one of the main attractions is the eighteen-hole golf course running down the middle of the spit. Canals paralleling the fairways form water hazards. This is a first-class, year-round public course with a complete pro shop, locker rooms, and dining facilities.

When you are not busy fishing, bicycling, or golfing, you can try swimming and sunning, either on the beach or in the Gull's diamond-shaped oceanside pool. A glass-paneled fence around the pool perimeter protects sunbathers from the breeze. The Gull also has an indoor sauna.

Dining

The well-equipped kitchens at the Grey Gull make it easy to prepare food "at home." It is a pleasure to be able to perk coffee and fry bacon and eggs for breakfast—no need to dress or go out. Lunch, or even a work-free, steak-and-salad dinner can be enjoyed by the fire in the evening.

When visitors do decide to go out for lunch or dinner and inquire about the best place to go, they will probably be directed to the restaurant at the golf club, called, for no discernible reason, Misfit, Ltd. It is just a few minutes' drive from the condominium, it is open all year, and it is good. A specialty is razor clams direct from the local beaches.

Another place open all year is the little coffee shop of the Ocean Shores Inn at the main crossroads. The big dining room is closed during the week in the off-season. The rest of the year it does a lot of convention business. The meals are excellent, but very expensive. The specialty of the house is big-name entertainment.

A new little restaurant, but already very popular, is the Onion

Patch. It is run by a young couple, recent refugees from California, who seem to know and enjoy their business. The food is gourmet quality and the service, to quote Grey Gull's manager, is "fantastic."

There are other small places along the beach, some with reputations for excellent food, but most are seasonal and not always open. An outstanding exception is the Ocean Crest Dinner House at Moclips, one of Washington's top restaurants and a full-fledged resort in its own right (see previous chapter by that name). It is a twenty-minute drive from the Grey Gull and is open all year.

Iron Springs Ocean Beach Resort

Distances:
   From Seattle—136 miles; allow 2½ hours
   From Portland—169 miles; allow 3½ hours
   From Vancouver, B.C.—281 miles; allow 5½ hours

Features:
   Secluded cottages with fireplaces and kitchens, in woods over-
      looking the ocean

Activities:
   Clamming, crabbing, swimming, beach activities, surf and
      stream fishing

Seasons:
   Year-round

Rates:
   $30 to $54 for two people; bookings should be made well in ad-
      vance for holidays, low tide periods, and midsummer

Address:
   Copalis Beach, Washington 98535

Phone:
   (206) 276-4230

Cabins line the bluff at Iron Springs

Iron Springs has been known and loved by generations of Washington beachcombers. Of all the getaways, it falls into a class by itself. Instead of being a big-building complex on a manicured landscape, it is an assortment of individual cottages scattered on a forested bluff above the ocean beach. Short, steep trails lead from the parking areas to the cabins and from the cabins to the beach. Tall, spindly smokestacks reach up through the dense trees so that fireplaces can draw, and there is plenty of wood stacked outside each door to encourage crackling fires.

The Iron Springs Resort has been around for a long time, and some of the cottages are getting on in years, showing signs here and there of age. But no matter. Their spaciousness, views, and seclusion make up for any minor imperfections.

Halfway between Pacific Beach and Copalis, which are pretty small places themselves, Iron Springs is "in the middle of nowhere." It is a great spot for family vacations—even the family dog is welcome. But if there were ever a place for two people to hole up and get reacquainted, this is it, too. When evening follows the gaudy Pacific sunset, profound solitude descends and there is nothing in the vicinity to interrupt it: no neighboring lights, no noise but the surf.

Routes and Distances

To reach the Iron Springs Resort follow the directions given in the Grey Gull chapter, except, upon reaching the coast, stay on Washington 109 heading north instead of making a left-hand turn to the south. The resort is on the left-hand side of the road, three miles past Copalis.

Accommodations

The Iron Springs Resort consists of a lodge or office building and fourteen cottages, three of which are duplexes. Put up at different times and placed to take advantage of particular terrain features or outlooks, each cottage has an individual character. Some accommodate four persons, some take as many as ten, and most will sleep six to eight.

Each cottage includes a big living room with a fireplace, a kitchen-dining room, one or more bedrooms, and a bath. (Filling a cottage to its limit involves the use of a sofa bed in the living room and no matter how many people sleep in a cottage, there is only one bath.) A woodbox outside the entry is filled daily with kindling and logs. Some cottages have doorside parking. No cottage is more than a minute or two from the beach.

Rustic decor predominates, with a lot of open-beam planked ceiling and darkly stained wood paneling. Furniture is typical summer-cottage style—of mixed character, but comfortable. The kitchens are stocked with cooking utensils and dishes, and the dining areas are furnished with plain but roomy tables and chairs.

No telephones or television sets come with the rooms, though as a concession to the times, television outlets are provided for guests who bring their own portables.

Summers, winter holidays, and weeks with low tides are usually booked solidly—up to three months ahead. Cottages are almost always available on winter weekdays, and cancelled summer reservations sometimes make room for spur-of-the-moment vacationers.

At least three days' stay is required for summer weekends, and one night's fee must be paid in advance to hold a reservation.

Activities

A look at the reservation schedule at Iron Springs reveals that, at any time of year, the periods booked farthest ahead coincide with the lowest tides. Pursuit of the wily razor has a high priority at this beach resort, and there is an abundance of other, more sedentary, clams. Check with the resort to get up-to-date information about regulations and seasons for clams and crabs. For those who come lacking the necessary tools, clam guns are available at the lodge for rent. On very low tides, crabs may be found in tidal lagoons around the big rocks rising from the surf to the south. The resort rents special rakes for catching crabs, but you might also want thick, protective gloves.

Rod-and-reel fishermen hold this stretch of beach in high esteem as a place from which to cast for sea perch and bass. There are also two freshwater streams on the property that sometimes yield good catches of cutthroat trout.

Iron Springs genuinely welcomes children and pets, and it is a perfect place for a family romp. The edge of the shallow creek running out through the sand is just the right spot for digging and building castles. Fires are permitted on the beach as long as they are kept away from concentrations of driftwood, and cookouts are fun. The tall, red bluffs that dominate the shoreline lend a special character to this beach.

Just behind the lodge is a freshwater swimming pool with a

Tide out on Iron Springs beach

diving board. It is heated year-round and covered by a bubble in winter. Across the highway, the Cove Gallery will supply art materials and lessons to painters and sketchers.

Many people ignore the beach activities and swimming and fishing and come just to hibernate in one of the cottages. They are quite content to look out through the spruce and other evergreens at the ocean.

Others come in the winter, hoping to settle down with a good fire and experience a raging storm. Sometimes they find their storm, but sometimes they end up walking the solitary beach with a warm winter sun on their backs.

Whenever you come, bring everything you will need to enjoy the beach. Plan ahead which meals will be eaten out, and bring supplies for the others. If you forget either the food or the equipment, Johnson's Mercantile is only three miles away in Copalis.

Dining

Iron Springs has no restaurant, so many guests come prepared to cook all their own meals and never leave the premises. Just to make it easier, members of the staff have adopted the custom of baking and selling cinnamon rolls in the morning and chowder made from local clams later in the day. Guests can perk their own coffee and pick up some hot rolls for breakfast and have chowder for lunch.

If, on the other hand, they prefer to eat out, there are restaurants nearby. Five miles up the coast, just short of Moclips, the Ocean Crest Dinner House stands high on a bluff right off Washington 109. The chef is a master of herbs and subtle sauces, and the menu includes seafood, beef, lamb, and chicken. A full bar and a good wine list are available. The dining area is divided into two small rooms that offer candlelight and dramatic views of the surf.

South of Iron Springs Resort, at Ocean Shores, the Onion Patch restaurant comes highly recommended as a place serving a limited menu of attractively prepared French–American specialties. Also at Ocean Shores, the Misfit, Ltd. at the golf course offers good food, drinks, and a pleasant evening. To the south, in Ocean City, the Surf and Sand is a clean, unpretentious restaurant with home-cooked seafood at moderate prices.

The area's restaurants are not at all "dressy." Casual clothing is adequate for this trip.

East-Central
Getaways

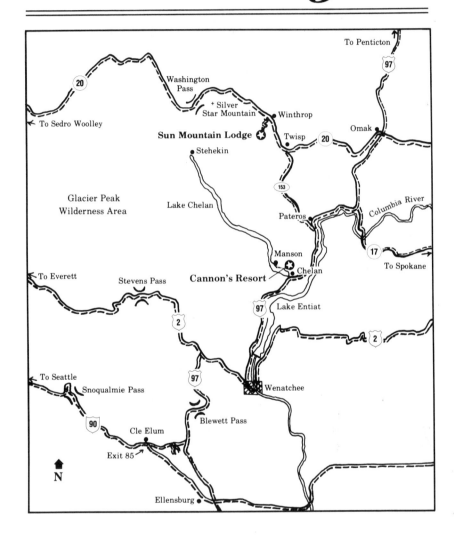

To Penticton

97

20

Washington
Pass

+ Silver
Star Mountain   Winthrop

To Sedro Woolley

Omak

Sun Mountain Lodge ✿   Twisp   20

Stehekin

Glacier Peak
Wilderness Area

Lake Chelan

153

Pateros   Columbia River

Manson

To Everett

Stevens Pass   **Cannon's Resort**   Chelan   17   To Spokane

97   Lake Entiat

2

To Seattle

97   2

Snoqualmie Pass   Wenatchee

90   Blewett Pass

Cle Elum

Exit 85

N

Ellensburg

Sun Mountain

Distances:

From Seattle—in summer 200 miles, allow 4 hours; in winter 240 miles, allow 5 hours

From Portland—400 miles, allow 8 hours

From Vancouver, B.C.—in summer 220 miles, allow 4½ hours; in winter 346 miles, allow 7 hours

Features:

Isolated mountaintop resort overlooking the Methow Valley in the North Cascades; above-average fair weather

Activities:

Horseback riding, tennis, swimming, fishing, river running, cross-country skiing, hiking, golf

Seasons:

Year-round; season A is high season, mid-June through September and the winter holidays; season B is May through mid-June, October through mid-November, and January 3 through February; season C is March and April

Rates:

$63 to $75 for two people, A season; $53 to $68 B season; $35 to $45 C season

Address:

P.O. Box 1000, Winthrop, Washington 98862

Phone:

(509) 996-2211; toll free in Washington, 1-800-572-0493

Winter scene at Sun Mountain Lodge

Sun Mountain did not get its name because there is lots of sunshine in the area, which there is, but because in the spring, when the balsamroot is in bloom, the whole mountaintop is one big mass of golden color.

After driving through the quiet, sparsely populated Methow Valley and up eight winding, empty miles to the mountaintop, it is always a surprise to come upon the sprawling buildings of the resort. How could anyone envision such an enterprise so far from major population centers? Yet Jack Barron, the grandson of an early Methow homesteader, had such a dream. His family's home had been the Sunny M Ranch on the valley floor. In the early 1950s, the Barrons converted the Sunny M into a dude ranch and Jack acquired a taste for innkeeping. From the ranch, he could see the far-off golden mountain and dreamed of building a major resort atop it—providing informal western hospitality, luxurious accommodations, attentive service, and glorious views without the modern intrusions of telephones and televisions.

In 1968, Barron acted on his dream, gambling that people would travel two or three hundred miles to spend a few days in such beautiful country. His idea paid off—the warm months from spring through fall were soon booked solid. But Sun Mountain is three thousand feet high, and in the winter when snow flew and temperatures fell, there was nothing for the resort to do but shut down. In 1976, aware of the growing interest in cross-country skiing, Barron took another gamble. Forty miles of trails were built over the broad, bare slopes and through the acres of wooded valleys, then a ski shop was installed, instructors were hired, and the lodge was kept open all winter. This gamble paid off, too, and Sun Mountain has become the only full-service destination ski resort in Washington—and one of the few in the West—that caters exclusively to cross-country skiers.

Routes and Distances

When the North Cascades road opens in the spring, it lops an hour off the driving time to Sun Mountain from both Vancouver and the Puget Sound region. At this time of year, Seattleites go north and Vancouverites south to Burlington, turn east onto Washington 20, go through Sedro Woolley, and through the two passes to Winthrop. This is beyond doubt the most spectacularly scenic drive in Washington. It closely follows the Skagit River past Concrete and Marblemount to Ross Lake, where three big dams—Gorge, Diablo, and Ross—come into sight. From the lake the road starts its long climb through mountainous terrain to the passes—first Rainy, then Washington, which at 5,477 feet is the highest in Washington or Oregon. At Washington Pass, Silver Star Mountain (a favorite of seasoned climbers) looms over the highway as travelers make the long descent to Winthrop.

If possible, plan to stop for a few minutes in Winthrop, an out-of-the-way town that has been carefully restored. You can capture the Old West flavor of the place in a stroll down the main street.

Just south of Winthrop are signs indicating the way to Sun Mountain. It is eight miles in on a narrow road to the lodge.

In winter, when the North Cascades road is closed by snow, the shortest route from Seattle is via Washington 522 through Bothell to Monroe. At Monroe take U.S. 2 east through Stevens Pass to the Peshastin junction with U.S. 97. Go north on 97 through Chelan to Pateros, then turn left toward Twisp onto Washington 153. Pick up Washington 20 just before Twisp. Eight miles north of Twisp and to the left is the well-marked road to Sun Mountain.

From Vancouver in the winter you can go south to Everett, turn east onto U.S. 2, and take the Stevens Pass route. You can also go east on Trans-Canada 1 to Hope, then on B.C. 3 to Osoyoos, and on U.S. 97 from here to Okanogan. At Okanogan take Washington 20 west through Twisp to the Sun Mountain signs.

The most interesting way to get to Sun Mountain from Portland is along the Columbia River to Biggs, then north on U.S. 97, across the river, through Yakima, Ellensburg, the Peshastin cutoff, and Chelan, all the way to Pateros and Washington 153. From here follow the Seattle winter route.

Private pilots can fly to the smoke jumpers' airstrip at Winthrop and call the lodge for transportation to the mountain. It is a well-maintained strip with a mile-long blacktop runway and no landing or tie-down fees. The inn monitors Unicom frequency 123.0, and will provide transportation within twenty minutes for pilots who call in.

Accommodations

At Sun Mountain, it is hard to take a good photograph of the main lodge building. Anyone trying to back up far enough to frame a picture is apt to tumble out of sight. But what is bad for photos is good for vistas, and the building is designed to take full advantage of them in all directions. It has big windows and cantilevered decking as well as heavy log framing and a great deal of dark woodwork. It is a style entirely fitting its location in the midst of mountainous western ranch country.

The fifty guest rooms, in two lodges separate from the main building, offer the same log framing and dark wood. Except for two special suites, all the rooms are alike. Each has a queen-size bed and two studio couches, as well as a view deck or patio. The rooms are spacious and comfortable for two. If the studio couches are converted to beds, four people can be accommodated in a room.

The two suites are at the north end of Gardner Lodge, positioned for panoramic views up the Methow Valley. They are roomy and comfortable, with separate bedrooms and fireplaces in the living rooms—a nice touch in winter after a day of ski touring. In winter, fires are also kept crackling for everyone's benefit in the big stone

Sun Mountain guests raft the Methow

fireplaces in the lodge lobby and the Eagle's Nest Lounge.

Activities

Sun Mountain has two seasons: warm, sunny summers and cold, clear winters. In summer the most popular activity is lounging by the outdoor swimming pool. It is a pool that must be seen to be appreciated. Just steps away from the main lodge, its location provides breathtaking panoramic views of the North Cascades' highest peaks, many of them snow capped all summer long.

Next in popularity is horseback riding, the original sport around which the lodge was conceived. Down a steep slope a few hundred yards from the lodge is a big corral where riders gather to meet the wrangler and to set out on daily expeditions into the hills. Breakfast trail rides and other special events are also arranged.

The lodge has four well-kept, Laykold-surfaced tennis courts, and many people come to the mountain specifically to play tennis.

Of course, everyone repairs to the pool after tennis or riding. If they tire of that, other water activities include fishing for rainbow trout in Lake Patterson, just a mile or so from the lodge. Boats are available there for resort guests.

A fast-growing sport is drifting down the Methow River in inflated rubber rafts. These expeditions are planned by the management and transportation is provided to and from the river. Two types of trips, both supervised and guided, are offered: a scenic cruise through quiet water and a more adventurous trip through the swift waters of the spectacular Black Canyon.

About twenty minutes away, near the airport, is the nine-hole Bear Creek public golf course, with the impressive mountain landscape visible from every tee.

In winter, activity revolves around cross-country skiing. All forty miles of cross-country trails are well marked, classified as to degree of difficulty, and kept well groomed all winter. The grooming is performed with a special machine towed behind a snowmobile; it pulverizes ruts and ice formations, then smooths out the surface of the trail.

The ski shop on the lower level of the lodge carries a wide selection of rental equipment so that the uninitiated can try out the sport. All necessary equipment—skis, poles, boots—can be rented. Lessons for beginners are given every morning, and in an hour and a half the new skier can acquire enough of the basics to venture out on the trails. More advanced students can get lessons in telemark turns and other difficult cross-country downhill techniques.

Group cross-country tours are popular. One of the most delightful outings is a moonlight tour offered at least once a week. The tour is

Cross-country skiers on Sun Mountain trail

great fun whether the moon is out or not. Head lamps, a guide, and hot drinks are provided for a nominal charge.

Beside the large swimming pool is a smaller, hot pool kept at about one hundred degrees Fahrenheit under a plastic bubble—a favorite first stop for chilled skiers coming back from a day in the snow. After the hot pool they like to visit the Eagle's Nest for hot wine and to gather around the stone fireplace and compare notes on routes and adventures.

After dinner the Eagle's Nest offers live entertainment and dancing five nights a week during the summer season and on Saturday nights during the winter.

Dining

Anyone spending more than a few days at Sun Mountain will probably enjoy going into Winthrop for dinner, just for a change. It is only nine miles away, and some of its restaurants are intriguing. The Virginian (after the book of that title, which was written in Winthrop) is a quaint restaurant with a versatile chef who can cook Chinese or Greek, or whatever his whim of the night dictates. For hamburgers or pizza, try Three-Fingered Jack's Saloon on Main Street.

The best food anywhere in the area, however, is at the lodge itself. On weekends people regularly drive fifty miles from Omak to have dinner at Sun Mountain. For a place so far from any major population center, the menu is surprisingly sophisticated. Moreover, it delivers what it promises because the food is attractively served and reasonably priced.

The dining room in the main lodge has a display kitchen where diners can watch the meals being prepared. Like the rest of the buildings, it is built of heavy timbers with exposed beams and offers views of snow-capped peaks on one side and a woodsy, enclosed patio on the other. When the weather is good, meals are served outdoors on this patio.

Cannon's Resort

Distances:
> From Seattle—185 miles; allow 3½ hours
> From Portland—329 miles; allow 6½ hours
> From Vancouver, B.C.—266 miles; allow 5 hours

Features:
> A compact, neatly arranged, family-oriented resort on a sandy beach on lower Lake Chelan; most units with full housekeeping facilities

Activities:
> Swimming in lake or heated pool, boating, fishing, water-skiing, volleyball; golf and tennis nearby, with downhill and cross-country skiing in winter

Seasons:
> Open year-round; summer season (July and August) is always busy; rates are drastically lowered for the off-seasons

Rates:
> $75 to $90 for two people in summer, $90 to $120 for suites for four; $30 to $36 for two people in winter, $36 to $48 for suites

Address:
> P.O. Box 699, Chelan, Washington 98816

Phone:
> (509) 682-2932

Cannon's Resort from the moorage dock

You will know you've reached the right place when you spot the assortment of scale model artillery pieces scattered about the foyer of Cannon's. They make an appropriate display, because Cannon's Resort really is *Cannon's*. The friendly personal presence and attention of Bonnie and Don Cannon head the list of attributes that make this a delightful place to visit.

The rate card emphasizes the personal touch, suggesting that guests make their hosts aware, before arrival, of any special services they might require, because "we'd like to have all your needs met when you arrive." This means arranging baby sitting services or transportation to and from the airport, setting up tee-off times at the local golf course, providing moorage for your boat, or making reservations on Chelan Airlines for high lake fishing and camping trips.

The rows of colorful flowers, the bright green manicured lawns, and the cleanliness and order of the premises are further evidence of the owners' concern for the comfort and well-being of their guests.

A particularly attractive aspect of the resort is its compact layout and ready access to the things you need and the things you want to do on vacation. The beach is directly in front—just a few steps out the door from the lower level rooms. Moorage is alongside the beach, for those who bring their own boats. There are barbecues and picnic tables on the sand ready to use, and a complete grocery just across the street can provide supplies. Next to the grocery is a little bakery that opens early for breakfast needs, and Michael's Restaurant, with its lakefront patio dining area, is just steps away, directly above the swimming pool. The Chelan area is blessed with approximately three hundred sunny days a year, and no place on the lake is better situated for taking advantage of them. With beach, pool, and lawns all facing south and west, Cannon's guests enjoy the sunshine right up to the last lingering rays of evening.

The resort's compact arrangement helps make it an ideal place to bring children. It is easy here for parents to keep an eye on their children while they themselves relax, and the bulk of the accommodations are actually small apartments with kitchens and separate bedrooms, convenient for family use. The short but busy summer season finds Cannon's fully booked, mostly by family groups. At other times of year, and especially spring and fall, the clientele is mostly adults on shorter getaway vacations.

Routes and Distances

Most people coming from Seattle will take the Sunset Highway over Snoqualmie Pass to Cle Elum, and then U.S. 97 across Blewett Pass, through Cashmere to Chelan. An alternative route, the Stevens Pass Highway, U.S. 2, is a narrower road, but slightly shorter and more scenic. Things to look for on this latter route are first the spectacular mountain scapes near Index, then the rushing river in Tumwater Canyon beyond Winton. About halfway down the canyon, keep an eye out for Castle Rock on the left. In summer it will generally have several parties of rock climbers "nailing" their way up its incredibly steep faces. You can pull off the road onto a narrow parking area just below the rock and watch for a while. Next comes Leavenworth, also known as "Little Bavaria"; it's a good place to stop for lunch. At Peshastin, pick up Highway 97, which proceeds up the grand gorge of the Columbia, past huge Rocky Reach Dam, and through exciting scenery all the way to Chelan.

Coming home, instead of taking U.S. 97 out of Chelan, go north a very slight distance to State Highway 151 and take it down through Chelan Falls and across the Columbia to the east bank, then follow it south along the river back to U.S. 2, where you recross the river just north of Wenatchee. Route 151 stays much closer to the river than 97 on the other side, and is correspondingly even more interesting (if that is possible) through thirty-five miles of orchards and riverfront scenery.

Accommodations

There are twenty-two units at Cannon's, seven of them right on

Grass terraces front each row of living units

the edge of Lake Chelan, with sliding glass doors opening onto a small lawn area and clusters of bright outdoor furniture. Beyond that is the delightful sandy beach with swings, tetherball, and a volleyball set-up. The other units are in a two-level structure known as the Terrace Building, set back on higher ground and separated from the beach units by their own terraced lawns, which also have sprinklings of umbrella tables and chairs as well as a shuffleboard game. The arrangement is such that every accommodation in the resort has an unobstructed view of the lake.

All but four or five of the units are two-bedroom suites designed to be roomy enough for comfortable group or family living—which is important, since during the summer season (Memorial Day through Labor Day) the Terrace Building can be rented for no fewer than four nights and the Beach Building for no fewer than six.

The two-bedroom suites have U-shaped kitchens, with spacious dining areas and living rooms fronting on the view side and the bedrooms and bath behind, to make quarters that are informal and pleasantly adapted to beach living. You may wonder about the plastic basin and bath mat placed just inside the sliding glass front door: you will find these come in handy for removing sand from your feet when you enter.

The walls of all units are paneled in birch and the living areas have chunky, overstuffed furniture, good for lounging and watching television. The kitchen is spacious and fully equipped, or you can always cook your dinner on one of the handy outdoor barbecues and eat at a picnic table on the beach.

The few one-bedroom units at Cannon's are similar to the two-bedroom suites, but the kitchens are pullman-style, with no oven or dishwasher. Like the larger units, they have either a balcony or patio opening off the living area, are fully carpeted, have a combination shower and tub, and are air-conditioned, with each unit individually controlled by thermostat.

During the off-season months, from September to mid-June, rates are substantially reduced—up to sixty percent in the winter, with the third night free. This makes these resort accommodations less expensive than an ordinary motel, so that for anyone in a position to get away during this long off-season period, this is a bargain that is hard to pass up.

Activities

Humans can sometimes be a little lemminglike in their propensity for doing the same thing all at the same time. At Lake Chelan, they arrive in droves on the first day of July and fill up every available room and cottage right through until Labor Day, when suddenly they thin out, reservations are easy to get again, and the pace slows down. Yet there is no lack of things to do, long before and long after that two-month busy season—in fact, some of the prettiest times of year on the lake come during May and June and September and October.

In any event, busy season or not, the lake and the water and boats and boating are the center of attention all summer long. Boats, from canoes to powerful ski-tows, can be rented at the M & M Marina across the lake from Cannon's. Many visitors bring their own boats and use a launching ramp a hundred yards west of the resort, next to the Chelan Airways seaplane base, for putting them in the water. Then they moor at Cannon's dock, close to their rooms.

People water-ski, sail, fish, and use their boats for touring and exploring the lake. For fishing, Lake Chelan is one of Washington State's best producers, open all year for rainbows and silver trout, and classified as a "bonus lake," meaning double limits are allowed by the Game Department. Fishing is good all over the lake, but the lunkers tend to come from the far end, where the water is extraordinarily deep and cold. The lake is fifty miles long, so a fast boat is necessary to get up to where they are.

Speed is also useful getting far up along the lakeshore, past the

The Cannon's Resort beachfront on Lake Chelan

orchards and roads and other signs of civilization, to watch for wild-life. Once up into undisturbed country, you slow way down and cruise quietly, close in, to look for bear, deer, and mountain goats.

For conventional sport, the number one attraction is the first-class eighteen-hole Chelan Municipal Golf Course, only a few minutes drive from Cannon's. There are also two free tennis courts in a park within easy walking distance, and four more at the high school, about five blocks distant. (None of these are championship quality courts, but they are playable.)

Two unconventional activities becoming popular in the area are interesting to watch, even if you don't participate. One is parasailing, across the lake near the marina, where for $20 you can actually get airborne and be towed aloft in a parachutelike kite from a fast boat, until you eventually land in the lake. The second is hang-gliding from the top of Chelan Butte, the high promontory directly to the south of the resort. You will understand why this is an ideal location when you see it; it's a perfect place for a running launch and, with favorable updrafts, it is possible to glide for fifteen or twenty minutes before coming to earth far below on the lakeshore. The drive up to the lookout on top is a worthwhile experience just for the breathtaking 360-degree view of the Columbia River valley, eastern Washington, the length of Lake Chelan, and the Cascade Mountains beyond. It is a long, narrow, very steep dirt road up, however; do not attempt it if your car is not in good shape.

The "trouble" with Chelan is that there are so many things to do and never enough time to do them. Nevertheless, a trip up-lake is practically a necessity. Most people do it on the *Lady of the Lake*, a cruise boat that leaves early each morning from its dock at the lower end of the lake and gets to Stehekin just at noon. It stays at Stehekin long enough for lunch and to allow time for passengers to walk around and explore the area, then returns to make port back at Chelan around 5 P.M. This is a perfect way to see the wild upper end of the lake where it reaches deep into the snowcapped Cascades. A variation that takes a fraction of the time (but costs more) is to make the trip on neighbor Ernie Gibson's Chelan Airways. Or you can go up by boat and come back by plane; the Cannons will make all the arrangements.

Another side trip is to take Highway 151 out of Chelan down to the Columbia to see the fruit packinghouses at Chelan Falls and to observe the debouchment of Washington's shortest river where it tumbles (when the dam is open) through a steep canyon into the Columbia.

A few people come up to the resort in the fall during the hunting season to go for chukar partridge in the high meadows around Chelan Butte, or for geese on the Columbia. In winter, cross-country skiing is often good on the Forest Service roads around the lake and up on the Butte, and there is downhill skiing at Echo Valley on Cooper Mountain, which is less than fifteen minutes from the resort. Echo Valley is only a small operation, with two poma lifts and some rope tows, but it can be good fun. It is open on Wednesdays, Saturdays, Sundays, and holidays, and occasionally stays open for night skiing.

Dining

For a town with a permanent population of only 2,500 (but which more than quadruples in the high season), Chelan is fortunate to have such a good selection of restaurants.

Guests at Cannon's will find that Michael's, a newly established restaurant on the resort's premises, offers fine food. Michael's is named for the present chef, who came to Chelan from the Hidden Valley Ranch in Cle Elum, where he acquired a following among discriminating diners. You can enjoy a wide view of the activity on the lake while you eat lunch or dinner on the outdoor patio.

Campbell House Restaurant, just next door to Cannon's Resort, has an established reputation for excellence among Chelan residents and is well known to tourists who come to the area. It is located on the lower level of the historic old Campbell Hotel, a prominent landmark

The Chelan River—at four miles one of Washington's shortest

you can't miss when you enter town. The restaurant has a fine menu and serves three meals a day, seven days a week. In good weather lunch is served on a second-floor covered veranda, which is brightened by flowers in planter boxes and checkered tablecloths. Here, too, you can glimpse activities on the lake as you enjoy the meal.

A few miles down the road on the east side of the lake, Wapato Point has an excellent dining spot, the Ellowee Beach Restaurant, open to the public and under new management at this writing. It is reputed to be serving good steak and seafood dinners at moderate prices. The high-ceilinged, airy dining room overlooking the boating beach is a most pleasant setting.

You might also want to try the Cove Marina. If you are on the west side of the lake, you can drive to it; if you are on the east side, the Cove will send a boat to pick you up on the dock at Manson and deliver you directly to your reserved table. Since the restaurant is strictly a family operation, you may find that the captain and first mate picking you up in the boat are a father and son combination you will later recognize as your waiter and busboy. This establishment has a reputation for good food and a beautiful view, and the locals say it has the best steak in town. The seafood is also good, and every entrée is accompanied by homemade French onion soup and a green salad. Altogether, the makings for a great evening out.

South
Getaways

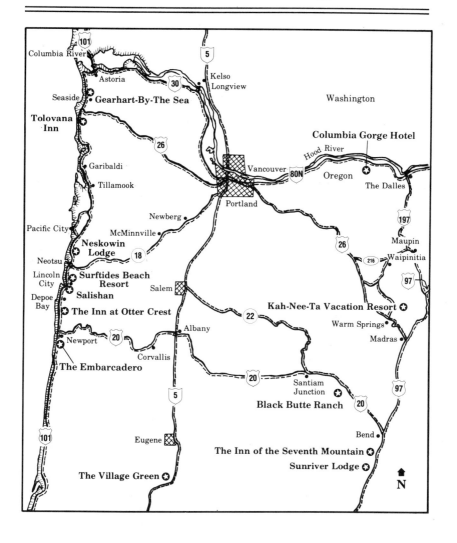

Kah-Nee-Ta
Vacation Resort

Distances:
> From Portland—114 miles; allow 2½ hours
> From Seattle—286 miles; allow 6 hours
> From Vancouver, B.C.—434 miles; allow 9 hours

Features:
> A large, complete, ultra-modern vacation complex set in a remote land of strange rock formations and multicolored canyons where the sun shines 340 days of the year

Activities:
> Swimming, mineral baths, golf, tennis, horseback riding, stream fishing

Seasons:
> Year-round

Rates:
> $42 to $67 for two people in summer; $30 to $52 for two people in winter

Address:
> Warm Springs, Oregon 97761

Phone:
> (503) 553-1112; toll free in Oregon, 1-800-452-1138; in other western states, 1-800-547-1102

Kah-Nee-Ta Lodge surrounds swimming pool

This large resort, standing way back among the unknown canyons of the Warm Springs Indian Reservation, invariably comes as a surprise to new visitors. They expect to see something unusual, but are seldom prepared for a resort of such size and elegance in so remote and improbable a location. The reservation encompasses nine hundred square miles, much of it dry, flinty, sagebrush land. Ages ago the southern part, where the resort now stands, was as flat as a tabletop. Today, fragments of the original ground level survive as the tops of the higher hills, which are identical in height. But the erosion of thousands of years has carved the land between them into a vast, rugged system of valleys and canyons.

Who would think such country could support life or be put to good use? Possibly it was the answer to these questions that prompted the federal government to give the area to the Confederated Tribes for their reservation.

As luck would have it, however, in time the Indians discovered a couple of things the federal government did not know. One was a stand of good pine timber beyond the broken country in the distant northern hills. The other was a spring in the south where hot mineral water came out of the ground.

Later, in more recent times, the tribes obtained a further settlement from the United States of several million dollars to go along with the arid land. The chiefs in charge of administering tribal affairs had the foresight to invest this money in two major projects. To take advantage of their good pine timber, they built a modern sawmill in the little town of Warm Springs. To take advantage of their sunshine and their mineral water, they decided to build a first-class resort.

The sagacious old chiefs hired topnotch architects and engineers to research and plan both projects. They budgeted enough money to do the jobs right, then hired experienced managers to run the projects after they were built.

The results stand as monuments to their thinking. The sawmill and logging operations provide employment and experience to hundreds of tribal members. The Kah-Nee-Ta Resort provides employment and experience, too. Because it is so conspicuously up-to-date, it also gives its owners—the members of the tribes—a progressive self-image.

Routes and Distances

Travel south to Portland from Seattle and Vancouver, British Columbia. There are two ways to get to Kah-Nee-Ta from Portland. The first and shortest is to take U.S. 26 east through Gresham, near Mount Hood, over the pass at Government Camp, and then down through the forest to the Warm Springs Indian Reservation on the other side of the Cascades. About seven or eight miles inside the reservation, begin looking to the left for a road to Simnasho: Kah-Nee-Ta is eighteen miles down this road. If you miss the turn, you can go to Warm Springs and take a road north to the resort, but this entails an extra twenty miles of driving.

When the mountain pass is closed, take the second route, which is fifty miles longer. This takes I-80N east from Portland to The Dalles. At The Dalles damsite turn south onto U.S. 197. Just before reaching the little town of Maupin, turn west onto 216 and drive to Wapinitia. Here, turn south onto the road leading to the reservation, Simnasho, and the resort.

Accommodations

The main lodge at Kah-Nee-Ta is built on a promontory above the Warm Springs River. The arrowhead design of the building gives every room in it a sunny exposure and an expansive view of the peaceful river valley and the sage-covered hills beyond. The rooms are tiered in three levels along the V of the arrowhead; the dining rooms and swimming pool are at the base, easily accessible from all the rooms.

The architects who designed the building used rich colors and textures and wood furniture, which complement the fine examples of Indian art displayed on the walls and along the corridors.

There are 114 lodge accommodations and all are spacious. Each has a deck, air conditioning, a telephone, a music system, and color television. There are two types of rooms particularly suitable for couples. The standard room has two beds, either double or queen-size. The deluxe accommodation is basically the same room furnished with a single king- or queen-size bed, leaving space for a sitting area with game tables and chairs. The latter is the most comfortable arrangement for two people.

Down in the river valley, barely visible from one end of the lodge, are the mineral springs, a huge hot pool, and a developed area called the village. For families, the village is probably the best place to stay. It has six one- or two-bedroom "Nee-Sha" cottages, some of which have kitchens, and rents for no more money than rooms up in the lodge.

Those who like to try everything have a fourth alternative—the tepees. There are twenty-one of them in the village. Each can accommodate up to six people and has a concrete floor with a fire pit in the center plus a picnic table and benches. Tepee campers must bring any other furnishings they need or want.

If you take your children along and feel they are old enough to be left alone, you can take a quiet room in the lodge and put them in a tepee. They will probably love it.

Package plans sometimes are available, some of them specifically for trail riding, rafting trips, or tennis or golf instruction.

Tepee Village at Kah-Nee-Ta

The nearest village for gasoline or groceries, Warm Springs, is eleven miles away, and it is a very small place. To be safe, try to anticipate everything you might need at Kah-Nee-Ta and bring it along.

Activities

There is a legend about how the mineral hot springs were discovered by Kah-Nee-Ta, an Indian woman whose name means "the root digger." She was an enchanting person, according to the story, which is, unfortunately, much too long to tell here. Visitors will hear it when they arrive. Suffice it to say that the resort was built because of the springs, and the pools and baths that use their water are still the major attraction.

The main outdoor pool is an unforgettable sight, bigger than two standard Olympic-size pools. It is in use all year, kept at just a bit under one hundred degrees Fahrenheit. In winter, when the weather is cold and snow lies on the ground, you see bathers frolicking in the water amid clouds of condensed vapor. Many people come to Kah-Nee-Ta for the beneficial therapy of the mineral water. For them the village provides individual hot baths.

The mineral water from the springs actually reaches the ground's surface at about 130 degrees, too hot for human contact, and must be cooled. The three sculptured Indian bears in the center of the big pool are really a fountain through which cool water is pumped to keep the water at a comfortable temperature.

There is also a regular swimming pool at the lodge. It is heated, but the water is ordinary fresh water kept at normal pool temperatures.

For guests who prefer the strenuous life, tennis, golf, and horseback riding are close at hand. Two well-maintained tennis courts are located at the bottom of the access road to the lodge.

Next to the tennis courts, spread out along the flat valley, is an eighteen-hole golf course. It has a pro shop with a teaching professional who rents out golf carts and other equipment. The tennis courts and golf course are closed during the winter, but it is often possible to play golf through November, depending on the weather.

This is desert country. To appreciate its vastness and get some sense of the problems and challenges that faced the people who traveled and lived here in Kah-Nee-Ta's times, you must venture out into it, away from the roads. Horseback was originally the only way to travel in the hills. It is still the best way to see the reservation's hinterlands. Guided tours of every kind and length can be arranged at the stables, just across the road from the village.

Since fly fishing for trout can be good in the Warm Springs River and its tributaries, fishermen might like to come with their poles and waders.

At the lodge in summer, people linger around the pool for a long time after dinner, enjoying conversation and possibly a beverage in the cool night air. Often there is live music and dancing in the Appaloosa Lounge; if not, there is always disco music and dancing in a room on the upper floor of the lodge.

Dining

Kah-Nee-Ta has two restaurants on the premises; because of the isolation they are where everyone eats. The Juniper Room in the

Famous Indian head rock formation near Kah-Nee-Ta

lodge is the main dining room. It is a lovely room with picture windows that look far down the valley and up at the hills. Like most of the rest of the lodge, the Juniper Room is an architectural tour de force. Arranged on several levels, its walls and ceiling are paneled in rich, mellow cedar, and the beamed ceiling soars to thirty feet. The food is as interesting as the architecture. The menu offers the usual meat and seafood dishes, plus such Indian delicacies as venison, buffalo steak, nu'sux salmon, and xat xat duck.

The dish that every guest should try is the "Bird in Clay." The bird is a cornish game hen, deboned, stuffed with savory mushroom dressing, and gently wrapped in Kah-Nee-Ta clay for slow baking. It must be ordered at least two hours in advance. A great show is made of serving the bird. It arrives at the table in a basket, still solidly encased in the hot clay. Each diner is presented with a wooden mallet to break open the shell. This takes considerable pounding but is well worth the effort. The persistent diner is rewarded by the heady aroma of the game hen and then by the moist, flavorful meat. Piquant wild blackberry sauce accompanies the bird. The mallets can be taken home as souvenirs for the kids.

Ilacxi sapi, Indian fried bread, is served with all entrées in the Juniper Room. It is very light and tastes like a cross between cornbread and a popover. With butter and blackberry jam, it is delicious.

The second restaurant is informal and is located in the village, near the tepees and cottages and the hot mineral pool. Called the River Room, it is perched right on the bank of the Warm Springs River. Its service is curtailed during the winter.

In the summer, beginning in late May and continuing through Labor Day, outdoor salmon bakes every Wednesday and Saturday are extremely popular and add an extra dimension to dining at Kah-Nee-Ta.

The Inn of the Seventh Mountain

Distances:

From Portland—167 miles; allow 3½ hours

From Seattle—342 miles; allow 7 hours

From Vancouver, B.C.—490 miles; allow 10 hours

Features:

Large condominium complex seven miles from Bend, near the Bachelor Butte ski area; dry, sunny summers; variety of winter and summer activities easily accessible

Activities:

Swimming, tennis, horseback riding, hiking, climbing, river rafting, fishing, bicycling, skiing, ice skating, sauna and whirlpool

Seasons:

Year-round

Rates:

$42 to $54 for two people in summer; $44 to $60 in winter

Address:

Box 1207, Bend, Oregon 97709

Phone:

(503) 382-8711; toll free in Oregon, 1-800-452-6810; elsewhere, 1-800-547-5668

Typical condominium unit at Inn of the Seventh Mountain

Majestic Mount Bachelor is the seventh major peak in a chain that begins with Mount Hood at Oregon's northern border. The Inn of the Seventh Mountain lies practically in its shadow, on the last piece of land before the Deschutes National Forest begins.

This part of Oregon is high desert country, over four thousand feet in elevation, with typically warm, dry summers (summer temperatures range from seventy to ninety degrees Fahrenheit) and only twelve inches of precipitation, mostly winter snow. The inn is located just where the desert begins to fade into the forest and the road starts its climb to the high Cascades. This is ideal summer-resort country, but proximity to the mountains makes it perfect for winter sports, too. Mount Bachelor has what is probably the best snow and finest skiing in Oregon. Consequently, the inn is one of the few vacation spots in the Northwest as much in demand in the winter as it is in the summer.

The weather is not all that makes this good vacation country. In an arc extending no more than twenty miles from the inn are thirty-three fish-filled mountain lakes, many rushing rivers for canoeing, rafting, and fishing, a wide variety of geologic phenomena, and endless trails for hiking, horseback riding, and climbing. Few places have such a range of natural attractions so close to comfortable accommodations.

Routes and Distances

From Vancouver, British Columbia, and Seattle drive south to Portland. From Portland choose one of two ways to get to The Inn of the Seventh Mountain; they take about the same amount of time.

The southern route follows Interstate 5 to Salem and then turns east onto Oregon 22. At Santiam Junction, seventy-two miles from Salem, the state highway merges with U.S. 20. Follow 20 east fifty miles to Bend. In winter it is prudent to check with the state patrol about driving conditions in Santiam Pass. Santiam's elevation is 4,800 feet and when there is ice or snow, chains sometimes are required. This scenic route passes Detroit Dam, the Mount Jefferson Wilderness Area, Hoodoo Ski Bowl, the 10,000-foot Sister mountains, and the lava-strewn desert area around Bend.

The other, more northerly, route through the mountains is east on U.S. 26 from Portland past Mount Hood and down through the pine forests into the desert country of the Warm Springs Indian Reservation. After leaving the reservation, pick up U.S. 97 at Madras and go south to Bend. In winter this route is heavily used by skiers heading for Timberline and Mount Hood Meadows ski areas, and the roads are usually open. But not always, so check on road conditions before starting out.

At Bend look for highway signs announcing Bachelor Butte. Follow them (along Century Drive) for seven miles to The Inn of the Seventh Mountain. The inn is on the left-hand side of the road.

Accommodations

Most of the units at this resort are studio apartments with fully equipped kitchens. There are standard and deluxe types. The standard studio has a fireplace, a kitchen, a private deck, and a queen-size Murphy bed. The deluxe studio is quite a bit larger, with the same features, as well as queen-size sofa bed, which allows the room to sleep four. Every studio has a television set, a telephone, and a free log for the fireplace. In addition, the inn has several kinds of family suites that can accommodate up to eight people.

If you rent a kitchen unit, plan to bring any special foods from home; a small convenience store on the property carries most staples.

Those not interested in kitchen facilities can choose between two styles of rooms. The standard lodge room is the smallest and least expensive. Adequate for two, it has a queen-size bed, color television, and telephone—but no deck. The deluxe lodge room is larger and has a private deck. With a Murphy bed as well as the regular queen-size bed, it can accommodate four.

The Inn of the Seventh Mountain is unusual among year-round resorts in that the rate schedule for rooms is higher during the winter season than in summer. Nevertheless, you can find economical accommodations here at either time.

Because summers and winters are booked well in advance, spring and fall are the best times for quick getaways; *usually* the weather is good enough for tennis, riding, and biking.

The inn has a variety of special package rates for people interested in alpine skiing, nordic skiing, rafting, tennis, horseback riding, and bicycling.

Activities

The outdoor swimming pool is heated all year. Close by are two outdoor Jacuzzis and a co-ed sauna. Snow may be heaped nearby in the winter, but that makes it all the more invigorating to dash from the dressing rooms to one after another of those warm havens. The pool area is physically in the center of the resort and in summer is the hub around which everything else revolves. Whatever else people do, they come back to the pool afterward to take a cool dip and relax in the sun. A second pool is opened up for children in summer so the adults can relax in their own area free from youngsters' commotion.

Tennis is played from spring through fall on seven new Plexipave courts. A pro gives individual lessons and also conducts ninety-minute group clinics every day. Courts may be used free by inn guests. Near the tennis courts is a corral with a big stable of horses and wranglers who guide horseback expeditions along the river or to local points of interest. Special rides, including barbecues and pack

Ice skaters at Inn of the Seventh Mountain

Seventh Mountain bicyclists passing Mount Bachelor

trips, are arranged whenever there is a demand.

Bicycles are available for rent or people bring their own for the popular new activity of riding fifteen miles up to Todd Lake near Mount Bachelor in a van supplied by the inn and then pedaling back again—most of the way downhill. It is a scenic ride on a road with relatively light traffic. Seasoned cyclists will shun the van and ride both ways.

Another popular summer sport is rafting on the Deschutes River. Transportation leaves the inn hourly during the day for the river. A short period of instruction is provided with a little practice paddling, then it is down the river—past meadows, lava beds, and forests, and through a few exciting patches of white water.

Rainbow and brown trout can often be caught in the river and nearby lakes. Also, the inn has its own stocked lake in which guests are permitted to try their luck.

Skiing and ice skating are, of course, the things to do in the winter. The ice rink is right beside Josiah's Restaurant. Skates can be rented at the rink, and an instructor is on hand to give both private and group lessons.

The inn is fifteen miles from Mount Bachelor's seven ski lifts. The mountain operates seven days a week from the first snow, usually in early November, until late spring. A warming lodge near the lifts serves breakfast, lunch, and cocktails, and includes a complete ski and rental shop. Lift tickets can be obtained at the inn. A ski bus operates on a regular schedule to and from the area.

The inn has recently added cross-country instructors to its staff and a rental shop of its own to outfit guests who need equipment. Clinics, transportation to ski areas, trail lunches, and waxing instruction are all available.

An important part of skiing everywhere is the after-ski activity. At the inn it begins, as the skiers drift back, in the saunas and Jacuzzis, then gravitates to the fireplace and conversation pit in the lounge. Later in the evening there is live music for dancing, and free feature movies shown nightly in the lodge building.

Dining

Josiah's, the inn's restaurant, has a reputation for serving food as good as any that can be found in the Bend area. The room itself has lots of color, with wood paneling, multilevel seating, clerestory windows, and high ceilings festooned with bright banners and hanging plants. Its bar and lounge are on a lower level, where the highlight is a sunken, upholstered conversation pit around a huge fireplace.

Josiah's serves three meals a day and is open seven days a week. Their special Caesar salad is served with all the dinners, which range from beef to chicken to seafood. On Sunday there is a more-than-ample champagne brunch.

After enjoying Josiah's dinners once or twice, you might like, for a change, to go into Bend where there are several restaurants worth trying. Cyrano's, downtown near the post office and city hall, is formal and quite elegant, serving preselected menus at just two sittings every evening. The food is very good and appropriately expensive. More casual is The Ore House, specializing in steaks and beef. Pine Tavern, closest of these to the inn, is recently remodeled and reports have been favorable.

Black Butte Ranch

Distances:
> From Portland—150 miles; allow 3 hours
> From Seattle—325 miles; allow 6½ hours

Features:
> Snowcapped mountains surround a region of lakes, meadows, and forest occupied by this large, completely equipped, comfortable condominium resort

Activities:
> Golf, tennis, swimming, canoeing, horseback riding, bicycling, skiing

Seasons:
> Year-round

Rates:
> $45 to $80 for two people; suites from $85, and private homes $100 to $125

Address:
> P.O. Box 8000, Black Butte Ranch, Oregon 97759

Phone:
> (503) 595-6211

Spacious Country Home condominium units at Black Butte Ranch

Black Butte Ranch is one of the most beautifully developed areas for recreational living on the West Coast. Its setting is a lush meadowland laced with spring-fed lakes, in the midst of a pine forest encircled by nine rugged, snowcapped mountain peaks. The weather in Central Oregon, dry and warm in summer and crisp and cold in winter, makes possible a variety of activities all year.

The many homes and condominiums scattered throughout this large property are all privately owned, with approximately eighty of the units in a rental pool managed by the Black Butte Lodge. A certain quietness and tranquility about this place, despite the number of activities, gives Black Butte the ambience of a private country club.

Summers at the ranch are family-oriented, with something for everyone to do. From Memorial Day through Labor Day, youth counselors are on duty all day at the recreation center to conduct children's programs, including arts and crafts in the morning and organized sports in the afternoon, leaving mom and dad free to play tennis or golf, to canoe, fish, jog, bike, ride, or just sit and enjoy the beauty of the mountains all around.

In winter, the pace slows down. This is a time for a quiet getaway, when you can enjoy holing up with a good book by a cheerful fire, or taking walks in the snowy pine forest and breathing the crisp, dry air.

This is not to say, however, that there are no regular winter activities. Santiam Pass is less than fifteen minutes away, and its Hoodoo Ski Bowl is considered one of Oregon's better ski areas, both for downhill and cross-country. Whenever the snow depth reaches six inches, the extensive golf courses and meadowlands are opened up to cross-country skiing on the ranch itself.

According to the wishes of the homeowners, the ranch is kept noncommercial and does no advertising. There is no charge for tennis or swimming or use of the canoes, and fees are nominal for golf, riding horses, and the use of bicycles.

Routes and Distances

From Portland, it is about the same distance to Black Butte whether you take the central route through Salem and Santiam Pass or the outside route via Government Pass and Madras. We prefer the latter because the magnificent open scenery of eastern Oregon never fails to stimulate a new sense of adventure.

If you decide to come by the former route, take Highway 22 east from Salem through Slayton to the junction with U.S. 20. Take this over Santiam Pass, and look for the Black Butte turnoff some fifteen minutes beyond the pass. The latter part of this trip is also highly scenic mountain driving.

For the outside trip, take U.S. 26 through Gresham, Government Camp, and the Warm Springs Reservation to Madras. From there take U.S. 97 to Redmond, where you turn right on Highway 126 toward Sisters. Continue through Sisters for about six more miles, to the Black Butte Ranch entrance on the left.

Accommodations

Rental accommodations are provided in three different condominium groups, as well as in a number of individual houses widely scattered on the property.

The most frequently used and most popular rental units are called the Lodge Condominiums, located near the lake and just a short walk to the restaurant and other ranch activity centers. Each of these units has been skillfully designed so that it can be rented as a complete apartment, comfortable for a party of six or more, or can be divided into three separate accommodations, each providing attractive quarters for a single couple.

The central units of these condominiums—and, of course, the most expensive—include a fully equipped kitchen and a tastefully furnished living room-dining area. The latter have high, lofted ceilings and corner fireplaces, and open onto decks facing toward a lovely view of the lake and mountains. In these units the bath, and bedroom

The Lodge units near the lake

with its king bed, are upstairs. These units offer a deluxe accommodation for two people.

The second arrangement, in terms of size and price, is the larger downstairs bedroom unit, which has its own cozy fireplace and private deck, also facing the view. These are spacious enough for a king bed, bedside tables, a pleasant sitting area by the fireplace, and, of course, a full bath—which has the nice addition of a percolator and fresh ground coffee for making that important first cup of the day.

The third component of each condominium is a somewhat smaller bedroom furnished with two queen beds, a couple of chairs, and a dresser and television set. The baths in these units are also smaller, having a stall shower instead of a tub, but they also have coffeemakers. These units are quite attractive and perfectly adequate for active people who do not intend to spend a lot of time in their rooms. Moreover, they are reasonably priced, being the least expensive on the Black Butte rate scale.

It is worth noting that renting the entire condominium is economical and convenient for two couples with their children, or three couples vacationing together, since each bedroom has its own private bath and the living room and kitchen are available for joint use.

The other two condominium units, one of which is close to one of the golf courses and therefore especially attractive to golfers, are not convertible into smaller units. They have two or three bedrooms, making them better suited for single families.

Activities

A large aerial map prominently displayed in the lodge near the registration desk gives newcomers to Black Butte an idea of the scope of activities available at the ranch.

Prominent at first glance are two championship golf courses on the opposite ends of the property. Both the Big Meadow and the Glaze Meadow courses are tough par seventy-twos, the former stretching out over 6,880 yards, and the latter 6,600. Each course is completely equipped and independent, with its own pro shop, snack bar, driving range, and putting green. Reservations are a necessity on all weekends and daily during the summer season.

Another open space that attracts the eye is the area of lush meadowland in the heart of the ranch. The lodge and the lodge swimming pool are here, located on the edge of a chain of little lakes that are popular with canoeists. The swimming pool lifeguard checks out canoes and life jackets at no charge throughout the day to those who want to paddle on the quiet waters and absorb the majesty of the surrounding mountain peaks.

The lakes are stocked with rainbows, especially restricted to flyfishing, and everything is kept sporty by the provision that only barb-

Mount Washington overlooks the resort's grounds

A network of bike paths connects the various lodgings

less hooks be used, with no baits or lures allowed. (The adjoining stream is a spawning ground for the trout and so is closed to both fishing and canoeing.)

A stable and corral can be clearly seen on the map on the eastern edge of the meadow near the entrance to the ranch. Owners and guests can rent horses here, and supervised trail rides through the forest are available on request.

You can see a Recreation Barn on the map on the other side of the meadow. This is the site of supervised activity for youngsters throughout the day and includes a basketball court, ping pong tables, pool tables, and facilities for many other organized sports.

Next to the swimming pool, on the edge of the lake, you will see four tennis courts. Looking farther, you will see more courts and pools near the golf courses and hidden in the woods. There are four pools and nineteen tennis courts, enough so there is seldom much crowding or waiting time.

The extensive system of trails winding through the woods and meadows and connecting all parts of the ranch is also clearly visible on the map. There could be no more beautiful and convenient place for jogging or bicycling. Bicycles can be rented by the hour or the day at the Sport Shop next to the swimming pool.

Other activities include hiking in the nearby Metolius area or climbing to the top of Black Butte itself (before winter snowfalls turn the whole area into a winter wonderland). Then, of course, skiing is the main activity, either at Hoodoo, only a fifteen-minute drive away, or at Mount Bachelor, an hour and a quarter's distance, or cross-country right on the property. For those who want to try the latter but don't have equipment, skis and most other sports necessities are for rent or sale at the Sports Shop, next to the swimming pool.

Dining

Meals in the lodge dining room are a delightful experience—which is a good thing, since for all practical purposes there are no alternatives in the vicinity. There are a couple of restaurants ten miles away in the town of Sisters, but none with food as good as that at Black Butte.

The dining room is rather small and intimate, staged on five levels so that the spectacular view of the lakes and the Three Sisters mountains can be enjoyed through the high picture windows from every table. The service here is fast and forthright, and the atmosphere informal enough that guests can feel comfortable in sports clothing.

Prime rib is the specialty of the house, but steaks, chops, and chicken dishes are available, along with seafood selections including oysters, crab, scampi, and fresh fish.

Soup or salad, a basket of ranch bread, and a beverage are included in the price of the dinner. If you are strong enough to resist dessert, you will nevertheless be served a piece of fudge with the coffee that is as rich as most desserts.

Breakfast and lunch are served in the same area and, like dinner, are served seven days a week during the summer season; the dining room is closed Mondays and Tuesdays in the winter. Lunch items and snacks are also available at the lodge poolside snack bar.

Sunriver Lodge

Distances:

From Portland—175 miles; allow 3½ hours

From Seattle—355 miles; allow 7½ hours

From Vancouver, B.C.—503 miles; allow 11 hours

Features:

Largest, most fully equipped, and one of the best-planned resorts in the Pacific Northwest; surrounded by national forest; sunny summers and cool, clear winters

Activities:

Golf, indoor and outdoor tennis, swimming, canoeing, horseback riding, bicycling, skiing, ice skating, racquetball, jogging, fishing, hiking, backpacking, nature tours

Seasons:

Year-round

Rates:

$42 to $64 for two people for lodge condominiums; $14 additional for kitchen units

Address:

Sunriver, Oregon 97702

Phone:

(503) 593-1221; toll free in Oregon, 1-800-452-6874; in other western states, 1-800-547-3922

Sunriver Lodge from golf course

People driving toward Sunriver looking forward to only golf and sunshine, good food and usual resort activities will be startled by the strange and fascinating geologic formations they begin to see along the highway seventy-five miles or so north of Bend. The whole Deschutes basin they are ascending is a wonderland of ancient caves, craters, lava beds, petrified forests, mineral deposits, and mountains whose tops are decorated by wierd spires and strange towers.

In the midst of this landscape is Sunriver—thirty-three hundred acres of basinland along an eight-mile stretch of the Deschutes—carefully planned and developed to preserve the delicate natural characteristics of the area. Wrapped around it is the Deschutes National Forest, which provides many recreational opportunities and protects Sunriver from other commercial development.

Because of its size and situation, Sunriver employs a full-time naturalist whose job is to see that the strict conservation guidelines of its founders are followed. His presence on the staff indicates the vision with which Sunriver has been developed.

The resort is set along the river in pancake-flat pine forest and meadowland. A portion of the meadow is used for two golf courses and an airstrip, while the lodge, the "Great Hall," convention center, the condominium units, and individual houses are carefully scattered in the woods. Miles of bicycle paths connect the far-flung development, and hidden in the trees, near the entrance, is a shopping mall filled with intriguingly designed shops, which supply groceries, gasoline, dry goods, gifts, sports equipment, fashions, and also include restaurants and a bakery; everything you are likely to need, in fact, for a week or a month's stay is available right on the premises.

The same is true of sports and recreation possibilities on Sunriver's own property. In addition, within a circle of a few dozen miles lie opportunities for other outdoor activities that range from rock climbing to archaeological exploration, from fly casting to white-water canoeing.

Sunriver is plunk in the middle of a thoroughly "natural" vacation area and is designed to make the most of it without harming it. As a getaway resort, it is the best of the best.

Routes and Distances

Get to Sunriver by following The Inn of the Seventh Mountain routes to Bend except instead of turning off toward Bachelor Butte, continue south from Bend on U.S. 97 for fourteen miles. Sunriver is on the right-hand side of the highway; the entrance is well marked. From anywhere in the Bend area, you can see the strange bare form of Lava Butte poking into the sky, its spiral road leading to the little observation tower on top. Once one passes the Lava Butte, Sunriver is but a short distance down the road.

The most expeditious way to get to Sunriver, if you can manage it, is by light plane. Out behind the lodge the resort has a paved and lighted airstrip that is forty-five hundred feet long. Fly in, walk to the lodge, and rent bicycles for land transportation. Modest tie-down fees are the only charge.

Accommodations

While at Sunriver, most getaway vacationers will stay in one of the lodge condominiums located relatively close to the main lodge and to the various activities such as tennis, swimming, and golf. There are 211 of these units, housed in scattered groupings of two-story buildings constructed of natural wood and rugged fieldstone.

The two most welcome features included in every unit are their private sun decks and their big fieldstone fireplaces. The decks are oriented to a woodsy outlook and the fireplaces are an invitation to feel at home and make full use of the room for relaxation. A generous supply of split logs and kindling is kept stacked outside every entrance. The rooms are spacious and tastefully decorated; they are furnished with comfortable king-size beds, game tables, chairs, and color television sets. Parking is adjacent to each unit.

A lodge condominium is just right for a single couple. For two or more couples or for a family, Sunriver has larger accommodations that are really full-size luxury homes arranged in groups. Each has a fully equipped kitchen, a spacious living and dining area, two or three bedrooms, and a patio or deck.

In order to preserve the natural qualities of the land, the housing groups and recreational facilities have been scattered widely over the resort's many acres. It can be a mile or more from one facility to another. Most people use bicycles or automobiles to get to and from the cluster houses, but walking gives you time and opportunity to appreciate the land.

Prices vary considerably at Sunriver. Ask the reservations clerk about current packages; and, if you want to play indoor tennis or racquetball, ask for a house or condo whose owner belongs to the Racquet Club.

Activities

There is no polo field at Sunriver, but beyond that it is hard to imagine any facility or activity it doesn't have! The natural terrain, the river, and the sun combine to make a beautiful playground, now tastefully and carefully augmented with man-made structures required for specific sports.

Near the lodge, the huge outdoor swimming pool has been built in the form of a mountain lake, complete with concrete lily pads for stepping stones. The gently sloping "mountainside" is ideal for sunbathing. A separate diving area and a special pool for children are also provided.

Nearby, a giant outdoor hot-tub deck contains seven wooden tubs, each with its own Jacuzzi jets. Often on a blustery, snowy day, tubbers gleefully soak with nothing but their faces out of the water.

For those seeking more active diversion, the only question is where to start. Eighteen tennis courts are located around the property in clusters of two to four, and the new Racquet Club houses three more indoor courts, plus five racquetball courts, a Jacuzzi, saunas, a lap pool, and a weight room. Two eighteen-hole golf courses, the newest designed by Robert Trent Jones, Jr., are laid out behind the lodge and among the condominiums. During the winter, when they are buried in snow, the golf courses become the center for cross-country ski instruction.

Downhill skiing remains the major winter sport in this part of Oregon. The snowpack at Mount Bachelor ski area will often reach a depth of sixteen or more feet, and the snow is typically light and dry—ideal powder. This ski area is just forty minutes away, and the lodge runs daily busses back and forth.

Eighteen miles of bike trails cover the lodge's meadowlands

A little lake on one golf course, right next to the lodge, freezes in winter and provides a handy skating rink. Skates can be rented, along with cross-country ski equipment, in a shop next to the lodge.

In summer, a pavilion rents bicycles. Bicycling is a practical way to get around the resort, which maintains over eighteen miles of smooth asphalt trails.

A marina on the banks of the Deschutes provides canoes and power boats suitable for river excursions. Fishing gear is also obtainable here. The river yields rainbow and brown trout to flycasters and fishermen using spinners.

Paddling the Deschutes in a Sunriver canoe

All-day canoe trips are a major attraction. The resort supplies canoes, box lunches, and transportation to points as far as twenty-five miles up river. These trips afford a memorable opportunity to become acquainted with the lovely Deschutes basin.

Near the marina are the stables, where you can get horses and guides and go exploring the nature trails in the resort itself or travel into the surrounding national forest.

Nature hikes and occasional backpacking and rock-hunting expeditions are led by the naturalist, who also conducts a running school.

There are regular wine-tasting demonstrations and summer music festivals featuring musicians from all over the country. In winter, Sunriver's community arts association exhibits over 100 winners of the annual Sunriver Art Competition at Sunriver Lodge.

Dining

There are nine places to eat at the resort, and each caters to a different mood.

The main dining room in the lodge is a large airy room with high ceilings and wood-paneled walls looking out over the golf course and a small lake, and beyond to the airstrip and the river. The food is consistently good, the menu varied, and the prices not unreasonable. The service is attentive and efficient. (At dinnertime, men may feel most comfortable here when wearing jackets.)

Next to the dining room is a less formal restaurant known as the Potter's Wheel. It serves hearty breakfasts and lunches daily, and on weekends is open for dinner.

During the summer, meals are also served outdoors on the Steak Deck, just outside the Owl's Nest Bar. You can choose your own steak or lobster, then sit back and enjoy a cocktail while watching a chef cook the meat over an open flame.

At the shopping mall there are four more eating places: the Casa de Ricardo, which serves Mexican food; the Tree House Pizza Parlor, where the food is inexpensive and plentiful; the Dough Factory, which features hot cinnamon rolls and coffee; and the Chuck Wagon, featuring avocado burgers, steaks, and salads.

The newest restaurant in the area is the Trout House, near the marina. Its offerings include salmon, Oregon scallops, and steak. Reservations are advisable.

The final place to get a bite to eat is the Sunspot Sandwich Shop, a snack bar in the "Great Hall," which serves hamburgers, shakes, and fries and is particularly handy when you are near the swimming pool or tennis courts.

Gearhart-By-The-Sea

Distances:
From Portland—83 miles; allow 2 hours
From Seattle—198 miles; allow 4½ hours
From Vancouver, B.C.—346 miles; allow 7½ hours

Features:
Oldest and quietest resort on the Oregon coast, but with new, rebuilt rental units

Activities:
Clamming, beach activities, swimming, bicycling, golf, tennis

Seasons:
Year-round

Rates:
$44 to $75 for two people

Address:
Marion Avenue at Tenth Street, Gearhart, Oregon 97138

Phone:
(503) 738-8331

Gearhart-By-The-Sea

The genial manager of Gearhart-By-The-Sea once said, "People come down here to do nothing. If they call ahead and ask, 'What is there to do when we get there?' I tell them, 'Nothing. Come on down and enjoy it!' "

That, of course, is not exactly true. Golf and clamming and other diversions are here for those who need something to do, but getting away from it all is the objective of most of Gearhart's dedicated clientele.

Gearhart-By-The-Sea is in a little community adjacent to Seaside. The two villages are as different as night and day. Seaside swarms with tourists in the summer. Its streets are lined with trinket shops, fast-food outlets, and stores with neon signs. The downtown part of Gearhart, on the other hand, is set well back from the highway, and consists of a modest grocery, a service station, an antique shop, and the city hall. One side of the long main street is lined with picturesque beach cottages; on the other side lie the quiet greens and fairways of the oldest golf course in Washington and Oregon. The broad beach, stretching in a gentle curve as far as the eye can see, suggests to the visitor nothing more strenuous than a leisurely walk as quite sufficient for a day's activities.

For almost as long as anyone could remember, Gearhart-By-The-Sea was an old shingled inn, a famous landmark on the Oregon coast. Then, in 1972, when it was on the verge of falling down, the inn was demolished by the wrecker's ball. It was a sad day for sentimentalists.

Now, on the same piece of ocean-front real estate, Gearhart-By-The-Sea has been reincarnated as a complex of condominiums. There was no way to recapture the charm of the original structure, and the new high-rise buildings may shock returning old-timers, but they will find compensation in new comfort and convenience. Meanwhile, the beach, the ocean, the famous golf course, and the quiet of the community—the things that have always been what make Gearhart something special—are the same as ever.

Routes and Distances

From downtown Portland take U.S. 26 for an easy two-hour drive west to the coast where it intersects U.S. 101; then go north six miles to Gearhart. Turn left off the highway at the Gearhart junction, go past the small group of stores, and turn right onto Marion Avenue at the tennis courts. Proceed about half a mile to the high-rise Gearhart House of Gearhart-By-The-Sea. The rental offices are in the pro shop to the right.

Travelers from Seattle and Vancouver, British Columbia, have several routes to choose from. The first is Interstate 5 (99 from Vancouver to the border) all the way to Portland, then the Portland route. But there are more scenic ways to go. The shortest and most direct of these is to turn west off I-5 onto Washington 4 at Kelso, proceed to Longview, and take the Longview bridge across the Columbia to Oregon. On the Oregon side, just past Wauna with its big pulp mill, stop for a minute at the lookout at Bradley State Park for a fifteen-mile view back the river along the route you traveled. Then follow U.S. 30 to Astoria, where it joins U.S. 101. From here it is a short twelve miles south to Gearhart.

For lunch on the road, two places to stop are the Country Cousin in Centralia (on the right-hand side of the freeway at the first Centralia exit) or Pier 11 at Astoria. A rooster crows as you go in the door of the Country Cousin, and the interior is loaded with country and old-time mementos. The coffee is good and the huge, hot cinnamon rolls are outstanding. Pier 11 is also well worth a stop. It is at the foot of Tenth and Eleventh streets, just a block off U.S. 101, in a remodeled wharf building. It contains a dozen interesting shops, a delicatessen for snack supplies, and a good restaurant with lots of window tables overlooking the harbor. In the adjacent lounge, lovers of woodworking will be entranced by "Cecil, the Sea Serpent," a life-size, twenty-five-foot fantasy made by a local craftsman from hundreds of carefully fitted pieces of exotic woods and without the use of a single nail.

Northerners with a little extra time might stay on Washington 4 through Kelso to Cathlamet, where a scenic little ferry crosses the Columbia to Westport and U.S. 30. Though not as fast as the Oregon-side route, Washington 4 is considerably more spectacular, as it follows the river closely, whereas Route 30 runs inland out of sight of the Columbia.

The fourth way to get to the Oregon coast from the north is to turn off I-5 at Olympia and take U.S. 12 to Aberdeen, where it meets U.S. 101. South on 101, after passing through Raymond, the road winds along the shores of Willapa Bay and the mouth of the Columbia until it crosses the high bridge to Astoria.

Accommodations

Gearhart has four separate sets of buildings in the new complex. The central structure is the huge, towering Gearhart House. To the north is the smaller but still imposing Pacific View. Scattered below on the oceanside are eleven low-lying buildings that make up the Pacific Palisades and Pacific Terraces.

The first-time visitor may have trouble deciding which kind of condominium to take. The important choice is between being able to see the grand ocean views and superb sunsets afforded by the higher levels of the Gearhart House, or being closer to the beach in the bungalows of the Pacific Palisades and Terraces.

All the units are decorated and furnished by the owners, so they are not uniform in appearance and all seem a good cut above commercial hotel facilities. The apartments at Gearhart vary in size and floor plan, but most have spacious living rooms, fireplaces (logs are delivered each day), dining areas, fully equipped kitchens, and either one or two bedrooms, each with its own bath. Two-bedroom apartments are arranged so that one bedroom and bath can be shut off from the other rooms and rented separately.

Rates vary according to location and the number of people occupying a unit. Two couples can comfortably share a two-bedroom unit, and the cost per couple will be less. One-night stays (during the summer and holidays) and pets are discouraged, although the management will sometimes make exceptions to both rules.

Activities

Since indolence is a legitimate pastime at Gearhart, a discussion of more strenuous activities may seem unnecessary. Nevertheless, if you feel like stirring, there are some attractive possibilities.

The beautiful eighteen-hole golf course, just across the street, draws golfers from all along the coast. Originally laid out in 1892, before the days of bulldozers, the course was built among natural dunes and carefully irrigated and fertilized for years so the right

The long wide beach at Gearhart

kinds of grasses could grow. It is a tricky course, playable year-round, and considered challenging and exciting by top golfers.

Quiet, level streets plus interesting architecture and scenery make the Gearhart area a favorite of bicyclists. Tennis players can use two well-kept public courts nearby.

The main attractions are always the beach and the surf. Right in front of the resort is probably the best razor-clamming beach in all Oregon. If you visit during a minus tide and decide to dig clams, *be sure you know the regulations and follow them carefully.*

Beach walking, looking for driftwood and floats, and shore-bird watching are favorite winter pastimes. Afterward, there is a good indoor pool to dip in and a hot spa back at the resort.

Dining

Every unit in the complex has a complete kitchen with pots, pans, dishes, and silverware, and most guests take advantage of this to prepare an occasional meal. For day-to-day groceries, a little store in Gearhart just a few blocks away carries most of the basics. One of the favorites for cooking is the excellent fresh seafood available on this section of the coast, which is a center of the fishing and crabbing industries. A reliable place to buy seafood is the Bell Buoy Crab and Seafood Store at the south end of Seaside on U.S. 101 just across from Rob's Restaurant.

If you prefer to dine out, the place to try first is the Crab Broiler (three miles south of Seaside, on the left, at the junction of U.S. 101 and 26). Inside, garden rooms and fireplaces greet you. The food is excellent, the prices reasonable, and the service friendly. If there is a culinary "must" for vacationers in the vicinity, eating at the Crab Broiler has to be it.

Other restaurants can be found along the highway and in the town of Seaside, within easy driving distance of Gearhart. Two of the best are Finegan and Company, a small, unpretentious place with very good food in downtown Seaside, and Hara's, across the street. Hara's is the opposite of Finegan's in most every respect. It is elegant and expensive, but the food is also top notch (try the "Crab Frederick"), and its bar is famous in these parts. Norma's, on Broadway, is popular for its seafood. It is open from mid-March through October.

Across from the Gearhart House is the Sandtrap Cafe and Bar. The cafe starts serving breakfast at seven and stays open until about three in the afternoon in order to serve hungry golfers. The little bar, which overlooks the golf course, stays open at night as long as there is anyone around, ordinarily until about one.

Tolovana Inn

Distances:
  From Portland—96 miles; allow 2 hours
  From Seattle—213 miles; allow 4½ hours
  From Vancouver, B.C.—361 miles; allow 7½ hours
Features:
  Resort on famous scenic beach; well kept up, comfortable, roomy
Activities:
  Miles of beach to walk, body surfing, swimming, fishing, horse-
    back riding, hiking, golf
Seasons:
  Year-round
Rates:
  $30 to $68 for two people
Address:
  P.O. Box 165, Tolovana Park, Oregon 97145
Phone:
  (503) 436-2211

Tolovana Inn

Driving down the Oregon coast along U.S. 101, the traveler is besieged by a succession of spectacular panoramas of headlands, beaches, and surf. One of the most striking is the long arc of Cannon Beach, punctuated by Haystack Rock and lesser monoliths rising dramatically out of the sea.

Tolovana Inn lies on the beach, laid out to secure the best possible view of Haystack Rock. The beach is table-flat and so hard that vehicles are allowed to drive on it in winter. It stretches in either direction from the inn as far as any jogger or walker is likely to travel.

Although summer is the most popular time for visiting the beach resorts, it is a mistake to overlook Tolovana in the winter. You can sit for hours by the fire, watching the huge waves uncoil and roar right below the window while the wind shrieks and rain goes by in horizontal sheets. Even then the ever-present gulls keep up their patrol above the water's edge, standing still in the air when they face the wind, then turning to swoop away at unbelievable speed.

Like Gearhart to the north, Cannon Beach Village is well away from the highway, and thus largely bypassed by the garish commercialism that blights so many beachside communities. Its little shops and stores are picturesque and invite the browser. On the side streets and beach frontage that constitute the rest of town, there is innovative cottage architecture everywhere to be discovered and appreciated by the visitor.

Little Cathlamet ferry is scenic way to Tolovana

Routes and Distances

From the north or from Portland, approach Tolovana by any of the routes described for Gearhart. Tolovana Beach is fourteen miles south of Gearhart, so Portlanders turn south, instead of north, from U.S. 26 onto 101.

Accommodations

Four three-story, fieldstone-and-cedar buildings make up Tolovana Inn. Except for the "mountain-view" units, the guest quarters are actually small apartments, in three different sizes, all attractively and comfortably furnished.

The smallest apartment is the studio unit—one large room with a fireplace and a private view balcony. It also has a queen-size hideaway bed or twin convertible sofas, a color television, and a well-equipped kitchen.

Next in size are one-bedroom units, which are just like the studio plus an additional bedroom. These are particularly comfortable for a couple. Four people can fit if the hideaway bed is used, although this can be a little crowded.

The largest unit follows the same basic plan but with two bedrooms and an additional bath. It is just right for four, but, again, six can crowd in.

Guests making reservations at Tolovana for the first time will be asked if they prefer oceanside or ocean-view units. Oceanside rooms look directly at the beach, which lies right under their balconies. These are the units for storm watchers. They cost a few dollars more than the ocean-view units; the latter are farther from the beach, but angled to provide nice views.

Guests on a budget can try a mountain-view unit, which is the back bedroom and bath of a two-bedroom unit, rented separately. It is comfortable and pleasant but has no fireplace, kitchen, or balcony.

Every guest unit has its own exterior entrance, and a Portland newspaper is deposited outside your door every morning. Coin-operated washer-dryers are located in the basement of one building.

This is a very popular resort. Summer reservations should be made two months in advance. Even in winter the weekends are usually filled and advance reservations are advisable. A weekend must be booked for at least two nights. During the week in winter, last-minute arrangements can usually be made.

Activities

At any ocean resort the beach is the thing, and Tolovana Inn is no exception. With miles of white sand to tramp in sunshine or rain, other activities hardly seem necessary. Beach walking in the summer is best done barefoot. In winter, walking shoes are necessary, although sneakers will do. Determined wintertime beach walkers and Japanese float hunters should have thick sweaters or warm jackets and hooded raingear.

The ocean is always cold, but in warm weather hardy types can be seen body surfing and swimming through the breakers. For others the inn provides a year-round indoor pool and a modern Jacuzzi set among an array of plants in a solarium. A sauna and dressing rooms are housed in the same building, along with an area for table tennis, a pool table, and some coin-operated games.

Deep-sea fishing charters are available at Warrenton and Garibaldi. During the summer, horses can be rented in Cannon Beach for regular trail rides or excursions on the hard sand of the beach.

For those not satisfied just tramping the beach, there is a good hiking area about ten miles to the northeast in Saddle Mountain State Park and an especially exhilarating trek across Tillamook Head, between Cannon Beach and Seaside. At the point where this trail reaches its highest elevation, you will be standing twelve hundred feet above the ocean, looking over spectacular views to both north and south.

Early fall is a good time to do the Tillamook Head trail because the mud often encountered in spring and summer is no longer a

Jogger passes the Haystack near Tolovana on a misty day

problem and the weather is more reliable. The trail's southern head is reached by driving three and a half miles through Ecola State Park just north of Cannon Beach to the Indian Beach parking area. Arrange to have someone pick you up at the trail's north terminus, or leave a car at that end of the trail.

Golfers will find a regulation eighteen-hole public course at Gearhart and a small nine-hole course at Seaside.

For nighttime diversion, the cozy lounge in the restaurant next door offers live music on Thursday, Friday, and Saturday evenings in summer and Friday and Saturday evenings in winter.

Dining

Management of the old Haystack House restaurant at Tolovana has been taken over by the Daggett family, well known on the Oregon coast since 1926 as operators of the celebrated Crab Broiler at Cannon Beach Junction. The new name of the restaurant at Tolovana is, appropriately, Daggett's, and as those familiar with the Crab Broiler would expect, the food, service, and decor are first-rate. The restaurant and bar have been extensively redecorated, though the old fieldstone fireplace remains the center of attraction. Outside, the same breathtaking views of the ocean, the famous Haystack, and the other Cannon Beach rock formations lie right beyond the restaurant's windows. In winter, when it is dark during the dinner hour, the ocean disappears in the blackness, but a fire in the fireplace provides a cheerful focal point. The restaurant opens at 11:30 A.M. and offers a changing menu with weekly specialties and a variety of fresh seafood according to the season.

For breakfast you can use your kitchen to prepare your own meal, or take the short drive into town to the Lemon Tree, which opens early.

Other places for dinner at Cannon Beach include the Whaler and the Driftwood Inn across the street. For quick, inexpensive meals, try the Pizza Vendor, an attractive restaurant directly across the highway from Tolovana Inn. You can eat on the premises or take food out. It is not too far to drive to the Crab Broiler itself, and a little farther on, at Seaside, Hara's is the best of a number of restaurants to choose from.

Columbia Gorge Hotel

Distances:
>   From Seattle—230 miles; allow 4½ hours
>   From Portland—66 miles; allow 1¼ hours

Features:
>   A historic hotel, restored and refurbished, on a site commanding panoramic views of the mighty Columbia; much favored for romantic weekend getaways

Activities:
>   Sightseeing and scenic drives in an area acknowledged to be one of the most beautiful in the Northwest; golf nearby, winter skiing at Mount Hood Meadows, water sports on the Columbia.

Seasons:
>   Year-round

Rates:
> $48 to $84 for two people weekdays; $60 to $96 weekends; all rates include the hotel's famous farm breakfast

Address:
>   4000 West Cliff Drive, Hood River, Oregon 97031

Phone:
>   (503) 386-5566

Ornate stonemasonry on the stately hotel's grounds

The things that make the Columbia Gorge Hotel special are old-time charm, a cliff-hanging location, and handy proximity to Portland for the quick getaway.

Simon Benson, a Norwegian immigrant who made a fortune in Oregon's early logging industry, developed an understandably strong desire to boost his adopted state, which he felt was the most beautiful in the union. He built the landmark Benson Hotel in Portland and later became chairman of the Oregon Highway Commission, where he was instrumental in pushing through the Columbia Gorge Highway to Hood River.

There he discovered an old frame building occupying a spectacular site over a high waterfall, directly beside his new highway: a perfect place for another hotel that could become a magnet to attract tourists into Oregon. He bought the property, tore down the wood building, and in its place in the year 1921 erected an elegant, super-substantial concrete hotel designed with every known convenience, including private baths attached to every bedroom. He hired the famous restaurateur, Henry Thiele, to manage it, and the Columbia Gorge Hotel quickly became the pride and center of Hood River society.

Over the years since then it has had its ups and downs, but the rock-solid building itself shows little sign of age. Now it has new owners, proprietors of the widely admired and successful Snoqualmie Falls Lodge of Washington State, who have devoted a great deal of time, expense, and experience to extensive interior redecoration and refurbishment. The results are an admirable complement to the tradition and history of the hotel. The lobby, which doubles in the old way as a cocktail lounge, is filled with comfortable antiques in attractive groupings. The original marble-topped check-in counter is still in place. Outside, the grounds are filled with lawns and flower beds and bridges over the meandering stream that terminates in Wah-Gwin-Gwin Falls.

People come to Columbia Gorge now to enjoy these things and escape the pressures of daily life. They look on it as a sanctuary where they can relax, eat well, and wind down to a slower pace. You will see the grounds dotted with small groups of people strolling about, gazing across the river at the distant shore, examining the remarkable old stonework forming the safety wall at the very edge of the cliff, and contemplating the falls that seem to emanate from just below the inn itself.

All this should make it plain that the Columbia Gorge Hotel is unique. Strenuous sports and organized diversions are for other times and other places and a different kind of resort. This one goes its own way, and in doing so seems to fill a niche many people need.

A stream bisects the grounds ending in Wha-Gwin-Gwin Falls

Routes and Distances

From Portland, go east on Interstate 84 to Hood River and take the first Hood River exit, 62, onto West Cliff Drive. Turn left on West Cliff. The hotel entrance is but a hundred yards along this road.

Even on the interstate, the drive down the Columbia Gorge is a scenic trip. It can be even better if a little extra time is allowed to take the old highway, now called the Scenic Highway, which branches from the interstate at exit 22, about twenty miles east of Portland. The drive goes past a succession of rocky cliffs, forest glens, and waterfalls, one after another, making it difficult to proceed without stopping here and there to look and snap a few pictures.

The other way to get to Hood River, and a delightful experience indeed, is to take Amtrak and let someone else do the driving. The train originates in Seattle, leaving at 8 A.M. from the King Street Station, and arrives at Hood River at 1:25 P.M., just in time for lunch. It is a pleasant, nostalgic trip, following the Sound to Tacoma and Olympia, past the Narrows Bridge, down the Centralia Valley, and along the Columbia to Kelso and into Portland. It leaves Portland at noon, and from there follows the Columbia Gorge, below the highway, right down along the water. There is a little piano bar in the lounge car and sandwiches are available. At Hood River, a telephone call will summon the hotel's equally nostalgic Cadillac limousine to pick you up at the station. The return trip leaves Hood River at 3:40 P.M., arriving in Portland at 5:30 and Seattle at 9:30 P.M.

Accommodations

When reviewing the rates for the hotel you should keep in mind that the farm breakfasts for two, included in the prices, are not just the ordinary continental coffee and roll, but rather a full five-course meal for which nonresident visitors pay eleven dollars each. If you like an elegant, leisurely breakfast, you will find this one a real bargain.

Another factor to consider is the advantage of coming midweek. Weekend getaways here are so popular that the rooms are usually booked solid well in advance, and the tariffs are correspondingly higher. Midweek prices are not only lower, but reservations are easy to make on short notice, and the staff has more time and attention for honoring individual requests.

Other than that, all forty-six rooms at the hotel are priced according to view, furnishings, and size, with most of them standard size. The least expensive of these standard rooms are furnished with a queen bed and overlook the garden side. A similar room across the hall, furnished in the same manner but with a magnificent view of the Columbia River, runs about ten dollars more. When these same rooms are furnished with king beds the tariff goes up another six dollars. All the rooms are comfortable, and all are equipped with color televisions and telephones, and have walk-in closets and charming old-fashioned baths, vintage 1920s, but with updated fixtures.

The rest of the rooms are large corner rooms with windows on both sides opening on spectacular views of the river and the steep hills of Washington. These are considerably more expensive than the standard rooms, but are very popular. They are furnished with romantic antique four-poster king beds with canopy tops, and a few offer the added attractions of a wood-burning fireplace and two comfortable high-backed, overstuffed chairs and a coffee table before the fire. Even though these rooms are the most expensive, they nevertheless are the ones usually booked first and farthest in advance.

Activities

Sightseeing along the Columbia Gorge, on both sides of the river and all around the lovely Hood River area, is the primary pastime of the hotel's guests. The scenic opportunities commence shortly after leaving Portland, whether you come along the river, or take the scenic route, which wanders inland from time to time along the way. The important thing is to allow as much time as possible for the trip. Some of the highlights to look for begin with the Scenic Highway and its succession of waterfalls, especially Multnomah Falls, the second highest and most beautiful falls in the United States, dropping 620 feet into a final treelined pool.

Farther along is Bonneville Dam, worth the better part of a day all by itself, with its attendant fish hatchery, fish ladder, locks, and extensive displays and observation facilities. Beyond Bonneville, you can cross the river on the Bridge of the Gods to the Washington side and drive back a short distance to Beacon Rock, a massive landmark said to be the world's second largest monolith, after the Rock of Gibraltar. A trail winds all the way to the top of the rock, providing spectacular views up and down the river, as well as making a fine place to take a picnic lunch.

Farther up, past Hood River, the Scenic Highway makes a loop back into pretty orchard country, where it rises steeply to Rowena Crest, which offers more fine outlooks up and down the river. On past The Dalles, at Biggs, another bridge crosses the Columbia to the site of the extraordinary Maryhill Museum, standing alone on a bleak hillside. Its collections include many Indian artifacts, Russian icons, and porcelains of note, as well as the country's most complete collection of Rodin sculptures.

There is a great deal more to see up and down the river, and there are a number of visitors' centers that will provide you with information and free literature. "The City Travel Guide" is concise and handy, as is the "Bonneville Lock and Dam" brochure, both readily available.

A few people might rather play golf than go touring. The Hood River Country Club Golf Course is just two miles from the hotel on Country Club Road, which is just on the other side of the overpass over the freeway. It is small, just nine holes, but is a pleasant course to play.

In the winter you can take advantage of one of the Mount Hood ski areas, about forty-five minutes from the hotel on Highway 35. One of them, Mount Hood Meadows, is more sheltered than some of the others and often has better snow. It is also the closest area to the hotel and is generally free of traffic hassles en route.

Dining

It is hard to say which is more impressive, the renowned farm breakfast or dinner, but overnight guests will have the opportunity to try both and form their own opinions.

Many people arrive here in the early afternoon when the Amtrak comes in, or after an easy drive from Portland. This allows plenty of time to stroll the grounds, look at the falls, and cultivate a keen appetite for dinner. This is important, because you will probably first stop by the lounge for an aperitif and the complimentary hors d'oeuvres served every evening. Then, when you go into dinner, you will find you have no more than picked up the menu when your waitress arrives with a whole tray full of appetizers: individual platters of avocado stuffed with shrimp, liver paté with crackers, stuffed eggs, salami, pickled baby corn, pickled herring, and a variety of vegetable rings. When you desist and say "no more," she will bring a kettle of the hotel's special split pea soup.

All this before the main course, so you must pace yourself because there are a dozen good entrées from which to choose. The rack of lamb, steak, prime rib, and fresh fish are all excellent. Dessert, like the appetizers, comes with the dinner.

Sleep well and long, because breakfast is just as challenging. Guests who have also visited Snoqualmie Lodge will find it similar to the breakfast that has delighted people for so many years. The first course includes blueberries, blackberries, melon slices, fresh strawberries, banana slices, and grapefruit halves. The second course is creamy oatmeal with brown sugar and cream. This is followed by fried eggs, hash brown potatoes, ham, sausage, and bacon—not one, but all. Hot biscuits come with this course, topped with apple blossom honey. Finally, hot cakes and maple syrup are served with the coffee to make sure you don't go home hungry.

The guest's biscuits are honeyed from shoulder height

For a dinner alternative to the hotel's own dining room, the Stonehedge Inn is usually mentioned first in these parts as the best local place. It occupies an old "country inn" building at the end of an isolated gravel road about two miles from the hotel. Open Wednesday through Sunday, it serves excellent food and cocktails, and the hotel clerk will explain just how to get there.

Neskowin Lodge

Distances:
> From Portland—95 miles; allow 2 hours
> From Seattle—270 miles; allow 5½ hours
> From Vancouver, B.C.—418 miles; allow 8½ hours

Features:
> Secluded, scenic ocean beach resort

Activities:
> Beach activities, surfing, swimming, golf, hiking, horseback riding, fishing

Seasons:
> Year-round; summer is always busy and requires advance reservations; fall is often uncrowded and is the prettiest time of year; winter is the storm watcher's season

Rates:
> $25 to $39 for two people

Address:
> P.O. Box 728, Neskowin, Oregon 97149

Phone:
> (503) 392-3191

Neskowin Lodge

Unsurpassed beach scenery backed up by a rugged ring of low mountains right behind the lodge describes the setting of Neskowin. This is a 65-room resort in a tiny community on Highway 101. The lodge is the community, in fact, except for one grocery store and the post office; and this may be the reason it is a favorite of Portlanders looking for a quiet and secluded getaway.

In terms of fancy architecture and elaborate facilities for recreation, Neskowin is quite on the unpretentious side. But it has light, airy, comfortable accommodations, with prices that are relatively low for both lodging and meals. It is particularly a place to come for those who are happy to entertain themselves.

The better rooms all have superb views, and it is only a minute from any of them out onto the beach, which, typical of this part of Oregon, is wide and flat and an invitation to long walks.

Neskowin is located in the middle of a stretch known locally as the "twenty miracle miles" of coast. The Siuslaw National Forest surrounds much of the area and, as described under "Activities," there are scores of natural phenomena with parks, trails, and drives throughout to be explored and experienced, no matter one's taste in such matters. It would take many trips to know this country really well, but that may be why it has so many "regulars" who come back time and again.

Routes and Distances

From Seattle and Vancouver, British Columbia, travel south to Portland. From Portland take U.S. 99W through Newberg to McMinnville, where it merges with Oregon 18. Follow 18 to Neotsu and the U.S. 101 junction. Take 101 north eight miles to Neskowin. The lodge, prominent and unmistakable, is to the left of the highway.

For a more scenic and leisurely drive from Washington, turn west onto Washington 4 at Kelso, go to Longview, and cross the bridge to Oregon. Take U.S. 30 to Astoria and then follow U.S. 101 along the coast. There are interesting sights everywhere along the way: Seaside, where the college crowd gathers each year to celebrate the rites of spring; Cannon Beach, with its monolithic rocks jutting out of the surf (take the Cannon Beach scenic loop from 101); and Garibaldi, where seafood is processed and the ruins of Oregon's first worker-owned plywood mill loom along the highway.

At Tillamook there are cheese and sausage factories that welcome visitors, and south of town are the giant balloon hangars from which antisub blimp patrols fanned out over the Pacific during World War II. Now these hangars house complete sawmills and plywood plants. They are so big—195-foot-high, clear-span ceilings—that clouds are said to form and rain fall inside when atmospheric conditions are right.

To see more of the coast after leaving Tillamook, look for the Three Capes scenic drive to Pacific City. This loop leads back to the coast through sand-dune country and tiny fishing villages. U.S. 101 heads inland for twenty miles of less interesting driving. The scenic drive rejoins 101 at Oretown, only five miles from Neskowin.

For an interesting lunch or coffee stop en route, see the section on Tolovana.

Accommodations

The big, three-story lodge building rests on the edge of Neskowin Creek at the point where it cuts its way through the beach to join the ocean. Just beyond that stands the Proposal Rock outcrop, surrounded by sea at high tide, but around which the creek must sweep at low tides, forming a deep channel in the sand. Waterfowl, gulls, and sea life of every kind seem to love this confluence of fresh and salt water, forested rock, and sandy beach, all of which are part of the constantly evolving views guests watch from their balconies.

Every unit, in fact, save for some low-cost hotel rooms on the nonview side has its own private balcony. If you plan to come in the winter for storm watching, ask for one of these rooms on the second or third level, which offer the best views and most excitement.

The unpretentiousness of the lodge is reflected by reasonable tariff schedules. The most expensive quarters are full one-bedroom suites with kitchens and two queen-size beds.

Next are a variety of sleeping rooms. The nicest are called "King-Bed-Deluxe" units for two. Then there is a "Queen-Bed-With-Kitchen" unit, also for two. Other rooms have two beds and can sleep four (should you not mind crowding).

On the highway side is the lowest price group, the nonview rooms, which have double beds. Most of these rooms, as well as some of the larger units, can be interconnected to make two- and three-room combinations.

Activities

Strolling, jogging, beachcombing, shell collecting, sunning, and surfing are all natural things to do here. The broad beaches stretch in both directions from the lodge as far as most people would care to walk or run. In summer a nearby stable rents saddle horses for beach riding.

Within walking distance of the lodge, which has its own game room and indoor swimming pool, are two nine-hole golf courses. Neskowin Beach Golf Club is an easy, level course open only in the dry season because it floods during the winter. Hawk Creek Golf Course, across the highway, is playable all year. It is a remarkably picturesque course that winds back up the canyon and presents many

Neskowin guests picnic on dunes near Pacific City

challenging lies.

Fishermen like to headquarter at Neskowin while steelheading on the Nestucca River near Cloverdale. Others find good fishing at the lodge itself, situated as it is at the confluence of Neskowin and Hawk creeks. When the tide is right—and learning to know the tides is the trick—sea-run cutthroat trout come up into the fresh water and provide some exciting angling.

Not to be missed is the Cascade Head Scenic Research Area just a short distance to the south. Because of the area's unusual ecology, ten thousand acres of Cascade Head were set aside by Congress in 1974 for joint recreational and research purposes. It is said that from the head's highest point, "you can see forever." Looking south the wide estuary of the Salmon River is a bright glimmer in the sun and beyond the rugged coast disappears into blue mists toward California. To the north the coast stretches eighteen hundred miles to Alaska.

You can explore Cascade Head on an easy five-mile trail. Eighty-year-olds have done it. Allow about five hours in and out and take a rucksack with bread, cheese, fruit, and wine for lunch. To get to the trail, drive south on U.S. 101 to the crest of the hill leading down toward Lincoln City. Immediately past the crest, look on the right for a gravel Forest Service road marked S-61. Follow this road for a few miles, bearing left when it forks. At the end of the road, park and take the trail. Plan to have lunch in the broad meadow high on the head. With luck you will hear sea lions barking on the rocks below. With field glasses you may even see them.

In the opposite direction from the lodge is another not-to-be-missed trip, the ten-mile drive to Pacific City. Go north seven miles on 101 to the sign that points left to the Three Capes scenic route. This takes you directly to Pacific City, home of the famous dory fishing fleet. The colorful dories are seen everywhere about town, parked on trailers. Most have imaginative and hopeful names painted on the sterns. Proceed out to Cape Kiwanda, where there is another prominent haystack monolith. This is where the dories are launched precariously through the surf during the fishing season from mid-June to Labor Day.

Behind the cape are towering sand dunes that are used all year as launching sites for hang gliders. Anyone who has not witnessed gliders in flight and appreciated the daring of their operators will not want to miss this experience.

Just beyond the hang-glider site, a short hike up a saddle of sand and onto the cape, spectacular views are available in both directions. Instead of sea lions, as at Cascade Head, you may catch seals sunning on the rocks below.

If the trip to Pacific City is taken at midday, bring a picnic to eat on the dunes or, for a treat, stop at the Dorymen Fish Company where you will be served a fresh crab cocktail and a little wine for an unusual and memorable lunch.

Another trip worth taking is the drive south of the lodge through old-growth timber in an ancient Oregon forest. Take U.S. 101 and the scenic drive that branches off it to the left. This route goes through the forest to the town of Otis. From Otis go west on Oregon 18 and then north on 101 back to Neskowin.

Dining

There is only one place to dine at Neskowin, but fortunately the food is good! The Golden Cove Restaurant is a part of the lodge complex and under the same management. From either the dining room or the lounge you see the creek, alive with gulls and ducks and leaping fish, winding past the windows to the surf. It is not unusual to see a family of otters playing in the creek or to watch long-legged herons standing in the water fishing for their own lunch. The restaurant offers a good selection of seafood and steaks at reasonable prices. The dining room and lounge are popular with the local population, so they buzz with activity even in the off-season. Breakfast, lunch, and dinner are served every day, and there is live music in the bar five nights a week.

For dining variety, Lincoln City is only twelve miles away. Try the Over-the-Waves restaurant at Surftides, or the Inn at Spanish Head. Both have top-notch menus and provide grand views of the ocean.

Surftides Beach Resort

Distances:

From Portland—95 miles; allow 2 hours

From Seattle—275 miles; allow 5½ hours

From Vancouver, B.C.—423 miles; allow 8½ hours

Features:

Large, well-equipped resort right on the beach includes covered tennis courts; indoor pool, sauna, Jacuzzi; gift shop and art gallery

Activities:

Tennis, golf, swimming, beach activities, fishing, browsing in Lincoln City's arts and crafts shops

Seasons:

Year-round

Rates:

$30.50 to $64.50 for two people

Address:

2945 N.W. Jetty Avenue, Lincoln City, Oregon 97367; mailing address, P.O. Box 406, Lincoln City, Oregon 97367

Phone:

(503) 994-2191; toll free in Oregon, 1-800-452-2159

Swimming pool building at entrance of Surftides

On the northern outskirts of Lincoln City, in a jumble of buildings crowding the beach, lies the Surftides Beach Resort. For thirty-six years it remained under the direction of the same owners, who continuously improved and expanded it until the resort is now one of the most complete, self-contained vacation complexes in the Northwest. Many visitors are content to settle down under its seagull-adorned triple smokestack and never leave the premises for nearly everything one might need or want is right at hand. The complex itself is made more interesting by the way the buildings are placed at different levels, connected by a web of narrow pathways, stairs, and boardwalks, all of which lead eventually to the broad beach.

Once ensconced in the resort, visitors are well insulated from the surrounding town, which is no thing of beauty, but nevertheless is the center of an area filled with attractions. The "twenty miracle miles" of coast, with Lincoln City as its hub, has fine weather, a great beach, and Oregon's finest parks and recreational areas. The city itself boasts more than twenty art galleries, and numerous studios where artisans exercise their skills of glass blowing, leather working, and woodcarving. Antique and gift shops abound, while dozens of restaurants, many of them good, vie for the visitors' trade. There are golf courses and fishing wharves and handsome buildings and rank commercialism—all randomly mixed in a way that appalls some and delights others.

In the midst of it all is Surftides, whose guests can remain tranquilly within the premises or venture out to pick and choose among everything the area has to offer.

Routes and Distances

Gleneden Beach, Otter Crest, and Lincoln City are all a few miles from each other and take the same driving directions.

From Portland follow 99W to Newberg and McMinnville and merge onto Oregon 18, which crosses the Coast Range Hills, joining U.S. 101 at Otis Junction and Neotsu. From Neotsu it is only three miles south to Lincoln City. Surftides Beach Resort is prominently advertised with big signs indicating where to turn off at the north end of town.

Accommodations

Most rooms at Surftides have large picture windows and a deck or balcony facing the sea. Why it is that watching surf has such a soothing influence on overstressed psyches is not fully understood, but it is known it happens, and these rooms have obviously been designed for the purpose.

Room sizes and rates cover a wide range. Some units have fireplaces, some have kitchenettes, and a few have both. Because of this variety, guests are well advised to ask the reservations clerk about the best quarters for their own particular needs.

Having been around for so long, Surftides sees a lot of second- and third-generation guests. People who stayed here as children are now bringing their own children. Many such people make reservations a full year ahead, so the resort is always booked well in advance for the summer season, although there are always some cancellations.

Major holidays are also booked well in advance. A number of people reserve kitchen apartments for Thanksgiving and Christmas and show up lugging their turkeys and trimmings to have a holiday in style away from home. Except for these holidays, reservations are easy to get in winter, even on short notice. Then is the time the fireplace units are particularly enjoyable, as well as a few dollars less expensive.

Activities

Resorts of every shape and size are straggled along the "twenty miracle miles" to take advantage of the area's popularity and its wide beach and clear skies. What makes Surftides stand out among them is the long-term dedication of its owners to provide a variety of amenities to complement the natural advantages of the sand and sea.

Even the most avid beachcombers enjoy occasional diversions. Surftides offers several, including an indoor tennis facility where guests can play in any weather. It has two top quality hard-surfaced courts plus a fully equipped pro shop and lounge. An instructor is on hand to help launch beginners or to work with advanced players on

Ocean scene from a Surftides' balcony

the fine points. Except for the one at Salishan, this is the only indoor tennis facility on the Oregon coast. There is a charge for using the courts.

Swimming is year-round at Surftides. The indoor pool is in a light, airy dome, which also houses a hot therapy pool and a sauna.

The beach remains the heart of the resort and is the main attraction. Strolling its length is pleasant in any weather. Beachcombers find interesting driftwood and occasional agates; during one recent four-day period, they reported picking up forty-five Japanese glass floats.

Surftides is close to some of the best fishing in Oregon. Deep-sea charters are available at Depoe Bay, and the nearby Salmon and Siletz rivers and Devil's Lake are steady producers of cutthroat trout and steelhead.

There are three golf courses close by. A sporty little nine at Devil's Lake is the closest, just a mile away. Hawk Creek is another nine at Neskowin, twelve miles to the north. More avid golfers will probably want to go a little farther south to Gleneden Beach to play the beautiful eighteen-hole championship course at Salishan.

Lincoln City's art galleries and crafts shops are usually hospitable to browsers who, of course, are always prospective buyers. One of the most interesting places to visit is the Sea Gull Factory, where it is fascinating to watch lifelike gulls being cast in concrete, then trimmed and hand painted until they are nearly indistinguishable from the real thing.

Last but not least is the nonactivity of winter storm watching. To be sure, this is a fine art, still practiced by only a few elites who understand the profits that accrue from relaxation with a good book and no telephones or interruptions, but plenty of time to gaze quietly out the window and contemplate life and values.

There are others, too, who come to combine a few days of storm watching with doing their Christmas cards, or taking care of accumulated correspondence, or preparing an income tax return. There are some things done better in peace when the pressure is off, and this, without doubt, is the time and the place to do them.

Dining

The Oregon coast is lined with good dining opportunities, but without question, one of the more memorable evenings a visitor can enjoy is dinner at Over-the-Waves Dining at Surftides. Built to jut over the sand, the semicircular restaurant allows all diners a 180-degree view of the surf and beach. At night floodlights shine toward the ocean, allowing everyone to see the foamy breakers rolling in. A new restaurant manager has done exciting and innovative things with the menu. His specialties are seafood delicately sautéed in butter and herbs, and prime rib served with creamy horseradish sauce.

A brief listing of the best nearby restaurants to visit for variety might start with Pier 101 on the beach, right in the heart of town. It excels at steamed clams prepared in beef broth and wine, as well as other seafoods, all served in a jolly and informal atmosphere. Next is the La Plaza, on the tenth floor of the Inn at Spanish Head, a fantastic vantage point for watching the sea. It features seafood and steak dinners and is popular for hearty breakfasts and lunches.

Henry Thiele's at the Dunes, north of Surftides, is an old establishment, well known and respected by knowledgeable Oregonians. Its reputation for excellence is based on family tradition with continuous operation under two generations of Thieles. Expect a pleasant ocean view and enticing menu here.

The Bay House, recently opened, is to the south, on Siletz Bay. It is small and intimate, with fine service and gourmet cuisine. Also new is the Dory Cove on Logan Road by the State Park. It is informal, with good, inexpensive seafood specialties.

Salishan

Distances:
From Portland—95 miles; allow 2 hours
From Seattle—270 miles; allow 5½ hours
From Vancouver, B.C.—418 miles; allow 8½ hours

Features:
Beautiful setting, landscaping, and architecture; top quality in all respects; covered tennis courts

Activities:
Golf, tennis, swimming, nature walks, beach activities, fishing, rock hunting

Seasons:
Year-round; May through October is the "high season"; lower rates generally apply other months

Rates:
$68 to $110 for two people

Address:
Gleneden Beach, Oregon 97388

Phone:
(503) 764-2371

Salishan rental units nestled in native trees

Salishan is the Oregon inn against which all others should probably be judged. It was conceived by Portland industrialist John Gray, who wanted—long before the environmental movement took root—to build a resort without seriously affecting the superb natural setting he had acquired. Experts in development scoffed at his plans and attempted to dissuade him. But he persisted, and his exceptional foresight has made Salishan a model of how nature and man's developments can work beautifully together.

Low lying and rambling among the native trees and ground cover, built entirely of Oregon fir, hemlock, and cedar, everything about Salishan is quietly and comfortably spick, span, and inviting. Nothing is ever allowed to become slightly worn or out of order, and each service the inn provides has been carefully thought out to make the visitor's stay a luxurious and long-to-be-remembered occasion.

If there is a drawback to Salishan it is only that, unlike most other coastal resorts, it is set a half-mile back from the ocean beaches. The beaches are there, of course, and available for guests to use, but it takes a fifteen-minute walk to get to them. The reason is exactly why John Gray contradicted prevailing wisdom. The beach environment in his opinion was too delicate to support such a major development. Only carefully spaced cottages are thus permitted on the beach, with all the other amenities kept at a purposeful distance.

Imaginative architecture dots Salishan Beach

To be sure, Salishan is one of the more expensive of our getaways, but the quality of the inn, the environment, and the experience there makes it worth every penny.

Routes and Distances

Follow Neskowin Lodge routes to get to Salishan Lodge. Go through Neotsu and south to Gleneden Beach. Salishan is to the left, nestled in an emerald hillside, impossible to miss.

Accommodations

Part of the charm of Salishan stems from the way the buildings have been designed to blend with the terrain. Accomplishing this, without disturbing the natural contours, meant that the 146 rental units are necessarily scattered over a wide area. Provision was then made for people to be able to walk comfortably in rainy weather—from building to building and to the lodge and tennis courts—protected by a network of rustic galleries and covered bridges. (Because of these distances, visitors whose primary interest is tennis may want to ask for rooms near the courts, while golfers may want accommodations closer to the links.)

There are just two basic room layouts repeated throughout the complex. Both are large and comfortable, tastefully decorated with their own fireplaces, view balconies, game tables, and ample sitting room facilities. The difference between the two is the fifty "Chieftain Deluxe" units are one hundred square feet larger to allow for a divider between the living and sleeping areas and they have their own small refrigerators.

Salishan is a popular winter convention spot for business associations, so it does not have an off season in the sense of some other resorts when nobody is around. Nevertheless, winter is less busy than summer. From November through April, excluding holidays, rates are reduced and reservations can be made less far in advance than during the rest of the year.

Activities

When we visit Salishan, we like to take along a basket of overdue reading and correspondence and hole up with it in front of a crackling fire, emerging only for a brisk beach walk in the morning and a game of tennis before dinner.

There is lots more to do than that, however, for those with more active tastes—following nature trails around the grounds, beachcombing, rock hunting, swimming, playing golf, going freshwater or deep-sea fishing, or even viewing the fine art collections in the lodge.

Strolling the beach at Salishan

The golf links are the highlight for some. Salishan's course, eighteen holes of immaculate greens and fairways, is playable year-round and held in high regard by golfers in the Northwest. There is a driving range and putting green, a complete pro shop, a golf professional who gives lessons, and a snack bar.

The one outdoor and three good indoor tennis courts at the north end of the complex also have their own pro shop and full-time teaching professional. Guests of the resort are charged greens fees and court fees for golf and indoor tennis. There is a smaller charge for use of the outdoor tennis courts.

A fifteen-minute walk across the highway and past the golf course leads to the narrow, two-mile long Salishan Spit and the ocean beach. From it you can see a host of wild creatures. Gray whales can often be seen in September and October on their way south to their winter grounds in Mexican waters, and in April and May on their way back north to their summer feeding grounds. Seals sometimes play in the surf, and there are always blue herons, egrets, ducks, and geese, and occasionally an eagle.

In the beach sand, new agate beds are constantly being exposed by the action of the waves, and rock hounds can also find jasper, pink granite, and a variety of blue quartz.

One special, not-to-be-missed feature along this unique sandspit is the fantastic variety of beach cottages. It appears that each new architect has tried to outdo all those who came before. A few hours of strolling up and down to capture the full flavor of this remarkable collection of buildings is well worth the time.

Walking shoes and warm clothing with a windbreaker are sometimes necessary for trips to the spit and beaches.

Dining

The lodge's elegant Gourmet Room offers a wide variety of excellent continental and American dishes. From appetizer to dessert, every item is prepared under the watchful eye of the certified executive chef and is exciting for those who appreciate fine food and wine. To feel comfortable here at night, men should wear jackets and women dresses or pants suits.

A second dining room, known as the Cedar Tree, is open for dinner from the middle of June through Labor Day. The specialties of the house are charcoal-broiled steaks, candlelight, dancing, and live entertainment. The Cedar Tree is less expensive than the Gourmet Room, and stays open until 1 A.M. for the benefit of night owls. The Attic Lounge, a cozy bar on the second level of the lodge above the Gourmet Room, also features live entertainment. On the main level, the Sun Room Coffee Shop is open for breakfast, lunch, and dinner, and has the best-stocked newsstand on the Oregon coast, including hard-to-find financial papers.

The Marketplace Mall, across the highway, has a number of interesting shops to explore, including the Marketplace Restaurant on Siletz Bay, which serves seafood, sandwiches, and steaks at reasonable prices. Not much farther away are the Sea Hag at Depoe Bay and a number of other good restaurants in Lincoln City.

The Embarcadero

Distances:
> From Portland—116 miles; allow 2½ hours
> From Seattle—291 miles; allow 6 hours

Features:
> Comfortable, well-equipped condominiums on the waterfront, each with a magnificent view of Newport's busy, picturesque Yaquina Bay harbor

Activities:
> Use of indoor swimming pool, sauna, and whirlpool bath; crabbing, clamming, deep sea fishing; sightseeing in Newport's Old Town

Seasons:
> Year-round

Rates:
> $49 to $75 for two people

Address:
> 1000 S.E. Bay Boulevard, P.O. Box 1067, Newport, Oregon 97365

Phone:
> (503) 265-8521; toll free in Oregon, 1-800-452-8567

Sun-facing roof patios at Embarcadero

Travelers driving through Newport on Highway 101 for the first time are apt to miss seeing the most interesting part of town, except, perhaps, for a fleeting glimpse of the harbor as they zip over the graceful old Yaquina Bay Bridge. Newport has grown apart into two distinct sections; the newer part, which they can't help but see, is commercial and garish, strung out for miles along the highway, while the part with all the charm, variously referred to as "Old Town," or "The Bayfront," is nearly hidden below the bridge on the north side of the bay.

From the bridge, however, if you look sharp, the one thing that stands out across the bay is a remarkable expanse of tiered gray buildings with windows cut into their roofs and a forest of tall, slender smokestacks rising toward the sky. This is the Embarcadero. You get to it by turning immediately off the north end of the bridge and dropping down a steeply curved road to Bay Boulevard which, despite its expansive name, is the narrow, crowded main street of the hidden Old Town section.

The Embarcadero is at the far end of Bay Boulevard, so you follow the boulevard the length of Old Town, glimpsing as you go the wharves, shops, boats, and fishermen—all of which you can plan to come back to observe more closely after you get settled. The resort's total modernity may strike you as out of keeping with the general ambience of Old Town, but you will quickly find that a mutual orientation to the waterfront ties the two comfortably together.

Like so many of the new resorts, the Embarcadero leads a double life. All of its many units are privately owned condominiums kept in a rental pool when the owners are not in residence, thus making them available to the general public. The advantage of these condominium units is that they are considerably larger and more comfortable than regular hotel rooms, yet no more expensive.

Immediately next to the condominium units are a recreation building and the main inn building, which houses the restaurant, lounge, gift shop, and registration desk. Below this are a banquet room and facilities for meetings and conventions.

After the unusual shape and arrangement of the condominiums, the most distinctive feature of the Embarcadero is the long, wide boardwalk that leads to the restaurant and fronts the length of the resort's extensive marina. It starts at the recreation building and ends at a store built over the water called Bait Shop, Beverages and Fish Market, where you can purchase almost anything needed to cook dinner or to catch dinner, whichever strikes your fancy. You are likely to fall easily into the rhythm of strolling along the boardwalk and out onto the docks to inspect boats, to watch the ducks and gulls, to see the herring jumping clear of the water, and sometimes a seal that may come right in among the boats. It is a routine that captures the real charm and character of this resort.

Routes and Distances

Newport is about one-third of the way down the Oregon coast, almost exactly due west of Albany and Corvallis. From Portland, take Highway 99 through Newberg and McMinnville to Oregon Highway 18, which leads to the coast at Neotsu. From Neotsu go south, through Lincoln City, thirty miles to Newport. Go all the way through Newport to the tall Bay Bridge and turn right just before the bridge. Signs will indicate the way to Bay Boulevard from there.

Accommodations

The tendency of all condominiums to look alike is broken by the unique design and distinctive appearance of the Embarcadero's dozen or more buildings nestled into the shore of Yaquina Bay. Their long roof lines slope gradually upward over three or four levels of buildings, with the decks of each unit forming small pockets in the shingled surface. It is a design ideal for wind protection and privacy, and one that positions every unit in the complex to catch the afternoon sun and to provide a magnificent view of the marina, the bay, and the graceful arches of the Bay Bridge.

The condominium interiors are designed so that each complete two-bedroom unit can be divided into two separate parts, either of which makes an excellent accommodation for one couple. The larger, more expensive section, called a "One-bedroom Suite" on the rate card, has a living-dining room with a sliding door out to the deck, a full kitchen, separate bedroom, and full bath. The living room portion includes a comfortable sofa and easy chair, a corner fireplace, television, and dining table with four chairs. This is a comfortable arrangement for those who plan to spend some time here and want to do some of their own cooking.

The smaller portion of each condo is directly above, with its own separate outside entrance. On the rate sheet, these are miscast as "Patio Suites." Whatever they are called, they are lovely rooms, each with its own deck and including a queen bed with a sitting area at the end of the room. They have no kitchen or fireplace, but are roomy and attractive, as well as being reasonably priced. (The couches in both size units open up to accommodate additional people, which is ideal for couples traveling with children.) The most inexpensive arrangement would be four people in either unit; for those who would like more space, the complete condominium, called a "Townhouse Suite," offers enough room to stretch out in.

Activities

Any time of day is a good time to go back down Bay Boulevard to visit Old Town. It is no more than a fifteen-minute walk, or you can drive in and park the car, then stroll up and down the length of the waterfront to savor the seafaring flavor of this original section of Newport. You can watch the commercial fishing boats unloading bottom fish, crab, shrimp, or salmon, according to their specialty, and catch glimpses of the processing going on in wharfside sheds. At one fishhouse, in the early morning you can watch through a plate glass window as a team of ten white-smocked women rapidly sort tiny bay shrimp flowing past on a conveyor. An eleventh woman carefully weighs the shrimp into gallon cans, which are then passed to a man operating a lidding machine. If you ever wondered where the makings for all those shrimp salads come from, this is it. Up and down the street, refrigerator trucks load the seafood for daily fresh delivery to restaurants all over Oregon.

Once the boats are unloaded and the processing houses are at work on the catch, the fishermen themselves gather in knots around the wharves to pass the time of day. They tend to be friendly folk, interesting to talk to if you want to gain a better understanding of their unusual and sometimes exciting way of life.

In the afternoons, you can watch the charter boats coming back,

Charter boats moored at Embarcadero's marina

or better yet, go out yourself for a five-hour or all-day deep sea fishing trip. One group of charters is based right at the Embarcadero Marina on the boardwalk, just a few minutes from the condominiums. The boats leave early, usually about 6 A.M., and it is advisable to make reservations at the little office on the boardwalk the day before. The five-hour fare is $35 and includes bait, tackle, and rods.

Another way to fish at the Embarcadero is to rent a crab ring for $3 from the Bait Shop at the far end of the boardwalk and go crabbing at the floating crab dock maintained for guests off the jetty by the recreation building. You tie a piece of bait onto the ring, let it down to the bottom of the bay for ten to fifteen minutes, then pull it up quickly with any crabs that have crawled onto the netting.

What to do with the catch? You eat it that evening for dinner. The rec building has everything needed for this in a special outdoor crab cooking shelter, including a big kettle on a gas burner, with counters and sinks and an instruction sheet on the wall detailing the correct cooking procedure. Full instructions for cleaning, how to determine keepers, and so on, are available at the Bait Shop.

You can also rent a small outboard at the marina to take clamming on the extensive tideflats in the bay, or just to tour the bay and the Yaquina River. No licenses are required for crabbing or clamming in the saltwater estuary.

Across the bay from the resort a group of buildings constituting the Oregon State University Marine Science Center is clearly visible and well worth a visit. The Center houses an aquarium and a variety of displays. Especially instructive, and of great interest to children, are "handling pools" where it is possible actually to touch, and thereby better understand, many sea creatures. You can even feel the slippery hide of an octopus, if you are brave enough (the sign says "careful, it can bite!").

Those who prefer golf will find the little nine-hole Agate Beach Course at the north end of Newport on the east side of Highway 101 the most enjoyable in the area.

What else is there to do? Visit the ocean beaches in nice weather, walk out on the North Jetty, just west of the Bay Bridge, to look for seals and rare birds, or use the resort's heated pool and hot spa in the rec building. In bad weather, build a fire in your condominium and relax with a good book.

Dining

Dining is a real pleasure in just about any seaport town, and Newport is no exception. The dining room at the Embarcadero itself has a spectacular view of the marina and the bay, and serves three meals a day in a bright, informal atmosphere. Breakfasts range from simple continental fare to exotic kinds of omelets. Good sandwiches

Swimmers view the bay from the enclosed pool and spa

and salads are available at lunchtime, and the dinner menu features standard meat and seafood selections. On Friday nights a popular seafood buffet is served, and on Sundays brunch is featured throughout the early part of the day.

A stroll along the bay front in Old Town will reveal a number of cozy spots where you can get seafood straight from the docks that day. Of all these, Mo's remains our favorite. It always seems to be crowded with jovial people enjoying themselves and the food in a cheerful, relaxed setting.

For those looking for a gourmet dinner in a more formal setting, Amerik's, just across the Bay Bridge, is probably the best bet. Somewhere in-between in terms of formality is The Center, a good restaurant on Canyon Way that has excellent dishes and in good weather sometimes serves outside in a quaint courtyard. Ask the desk clerk at the Embarcadero for directions to any of these restaurants—she will be glad to help you.

The Inn at Otter Crest

Distances:
> From Portland—108 miles; allow 2¼ hours
> From Seattle—283 miles; allow 5¾ hours
> From Vancouver, B.C.—431 miles; allow 8¾ hours

Features:
> Dramatic view of the ocean from a high-bluff setting; secluded beach and rugged coastline below

Activities:
> Beach activities, tennis, nature trails, golf, fishing, swimming

Seasons:
> Year-round; advance reservations usually necessary

Rates:
> Bedrooms or studios, $55 for two people; loft suites, $85 for two to six people; package plans available year-round which include lunch and dinner

Address:
> Otter Rock, Oregon 97369

Phone:
> (503) 765-2111; toll free in Oregon, 1-800-452-2101; elsewhere, 1-800-547-2181

The Inn at Otter Crest high on a cliff

Beyond a doubt, The Inn at Otter Crest, perched high on a bluff over the sea, commands the most dramatic setting of any of the Oregon ocean resorts. It stands above a stretch of coast that was discovered in 1778 by Captain James Cook, who promptly named it Cape Foulweather in recognition of the violent storms and driving sleet that prevented him from putting a party ashore. He finally was forced to sail away without the water and supplies he had sought, but the name he so bitterly bequeathed has stuck and the Otter Crest region still appears on maps today as Cape Foulweather. Visitors who witness one of the area's frequent winter storms will recognize the aptness of the name, but they have the advantage of being snug and warm by a cozy fireside while the weather rages outside.

Things are different in summer. The sun shines down on people engaged in a myriad of outdoor activities centering around the beach, the outdoor pool and broad lawn, two fine tennis courts, and a maze of woodland nature trails revealing the beauty of the undisturbed forest.

Routes and Distances

For the shortest route to Otter Crest from Portland take 99W southwest to Newberg and McMinnville, then follow state highway 18 to the coast at Neotsu where it joins U.S. 101. From the Neotsu junction it is fifteen miles to Depoe Bay. Two miles beyond Depoe Bay look for the Otter Crest Loop. It leads directly to the entrance to the inn. If arriving in daytime, try to allow leisure time to pause at the frequent turnouts between Depoe Bay and your destination. The highway hugs the coastal cliffs along this stretch and rises at one point to 450 feet above the sea. The turnout nearest the inn offers the best view. It leads to a Coast Guard station that has ample parking and a vantage point looking directly down upon Otter Rock, the roofs of the inn's sprawling complex, and a long, rocky coast beyond.

Accommodations

The rustic buildings that house Otter Crest's 250-odd units seem to be cantilevered on the side of a steep slope, giving virtually every room a dramatic view of the sea. Each building consists of a series of identical condominium suites that can be divided into two units. A complete suite provides ample space and privacy for four people. To provide smaller accommodations, the suites are partitioned, making two basic room designs suitable for couples. One of the halves forms a long, narrow room with two double beds, a color television, a refrigerator, and a deck. The other more expensive half, listed as a studio unit, consists of a living room with a queen-size sofa bed, a log-burning fireplace, a fully equipped kitchen, and a view deck. This is a more pleasant arrangement for two people. If you take a kitchen

Exploring tidal pools below Inn at Otter Crest

Tidal cave near Otter Crest

unit, be sure to bring all necessary food supplies; there is no store at the inn.

Activities

The mailing address of the inn is Otter Rock, Oregon, but in fact Otter Rock is no more than a fire station and a school; the closest real towns are Depoe Bay to the north and Newport to the south. The Inn at Otter Crest is, in other words, isolated, but it is also self-contained. Although guests may drive out to dinner on occasion, they tend to remain on the premises and enjoy what the inn itself has to offer.

As with all coastal resorts, Otter Crest's orientation is to the sea. A favorite activity, summer and winter, is to take the long flight of wooden steps down the face of the cliff and explore the beach below. Storms concentrate debris here, making it a good place to search for interesting driftwood shapes and other flotsam. There is also an abundance of polished, flat, black stones, which are fun to collect for household or garden decorations. Warm jackets and windbreakers are essential for off-season beachcombers.

Devil's Punch Bowl State Park is only a short walk away. A trail starting midway along the southern loop road around the inn leads visitors through the lush, green woods to the next coastal promontory, where they can spend some time looking at the churning waters in the punch bowl, then explore the marine gardens beyond.

A nice diversion is a lunch of fresh-from-the-ocean seafood at Mo's West, followed by poking around the pottery shop next door, where craftsmen invite visitors to watch them work the clay.

Farther afield, the Agate Beach golf course south of Otter Crest is one of Oregon's better courses and is playable year-round. Deep-sea fishing charters are available in season at nearby Depoe Bay. In summer you can play tennis, and swim in the outdoor pool. The inn also maintains a putting green, a sauna, and a game room.

Dining

The Flying Dutchman Restaurant at Otter Crest is perched on the last knoll of land before the cliff drops sharply to the sea. The dining room is wedge shaped, simulating the bow of a ship, and the large windows along both walls ensure a spectacular ocean view from any table in the room. The restaurant serves breakfast, lunch, and dinner, which includes local seafood, steak, and duck à l'orange. Next door, the Wardroom Lounge—a favorite whale watching station by day—features dancing and live entertainment in the evenings.

One of the popular features of the Flying Dutchman is the all-day Sunday buffet. It begins as brunch early in the day, with an elegant layout of fresh fruits, salads, and breads, then becomes a buffet dinner at twelve-thirty, when a baron of beef and various hot dishes are added. Guests enjoy helping themselves, at their leisure, to the reasonably priced food.

For variety an interesting place to dine is the picturesque little town of Depoe Bay, just a couple of miles north. Depoe Bay boasts of having the smallest harbor in the world and it is always jammed with colorful deep-sea fishing boats. The nearby Sea Hag Restaurant, whose genial owner and hostess—"Gracie"—is known up and down the Oregon coast for her hospitality, is a delightful place to go for either lunch or dinner. Gracie's Clam Chowder appears on the menu with the note that the *New York Times* called it "the best anywhere."

Lincoln City, a few miles farther north, also has several very good restaurants.

In Newport, to the south, shops and galleries intermingle with wharves, restaurants, and grog shops, making it an interesting place to explore.

The Village Green

Distances:
From Portland—130 miles; allow 2¾ hours
From Seattle—285 miles; allow 5¾ hours
From Vancouver, B.C.—433 miles; allow 8¾ hours
From San Francisco—498 miles; allow 10 hours

Features:
Exceptionally plush and comfortable getaway destination; outstanding service; good layover en route to San Francisco

Activities:
Golf, swimming, tennis, nostalgic train ride, bowling, pitch and putt golf; public golf course nearby

Seasons:
Year-round

Rates:
$54 to $58 for two people, with suites from $90

Address:
P.O. Box 277, Cottage Grove, Oregon 97424

Phone:
(503) 942-2491; toll free in Oregon, 1-800-452-8960; elsewhere, 1-800-547-8810

The secluded poolside at The Village Green

No ordinary hotel located in the kind of place as The Village Green could expect to be known as a destination resort. Situated in a small town with no need for a big hotel, and with no lakes or beaches or particular scenic attractions to otherwise lure visitors, The Village Green nevertheless maintains a constantly high occupancy rate and a top national reputation with a clientele that is sixty percent non-business.

The reason for this anomaly is simply that high, stringently maintained management standards have made The Village Green exceptionally pleasant for short getaways, and people flock to it from far and near. It is known as a place where you can expect to be pampered and waited on and to indulge yourself in the most comfortable and luxurious of surroundings. It could have been built nearly anywhere in Oregon and been as successful; it just happens to be in Cottage Grove because that is the area where millionaire lumberman Walter Woodward made his fortune and where he decided to build a great hotel as a tribute to the community that contributed to his success.

A tall, conventional building would have been out of character with the flat, green farms and forests of the Willamette Valley. Woodward's designers settled instead on a low, rambling, single-story theme in keeping with the Oregon countryside, and also in keeping, thanks to a network of covered walkways, with its well-known fickle weather.

The general theme of The Village Green is spaciousness and comfort and graceful living, but there are pleasant diversions for those who want them. In fact, it's sometimes hard to tell whether the inn is a resort masquerading as a hotel or the other way around!

Routes and Distances

Cottage Grove lies almost exactly midway between Portland and the California border. It also lies midway between Vancouver, British Columbia, and San Francisco (498 miles and ten hours from Cottage Grove). This makes it an ideal stopover for travelers journeying up or down the coast. With a bit of advance planning, a long trip south, even a business trip, can include a two-day respite at The Village Green.

Whatever the reason for traveling to Cottage Grove, there is only one route by auto: Interstate 5 all the way. Take exit 174 and follow the signs to the inn.

Owners of private aircraft can land at a small airport conveniently adjacent to the inn property. It has a good, paved, 3600-foot runway—lighted at night—and a special tie-down area for the use of hotel guests.

Accommodations

All 100 units are done in northwest ranch-style architecture with cedar siding and heavy shake roofs. The rooms are laid out in rows around the golf greens and overlooking the swimming pool. Every unit has two entrances, one at an individual covered carport, the other at a covered walkway that connects all buildings in the complex. The rooms are large and luxurious, each with a bay window and walnut paneling in the sitting area.

Even with all this, however, the key to The Village Green's success is the extravagant service. Where else is the bed turned down while you are at dinner and a little package of chocolate "good-night" kisses placed on the pillow? Where else do you return to the room before the cocktail hour to find an attractive package of cheese and crackers, compliments of the house? Where else is it possible to order champagne breakfast for the next morning—served in bed? And even with this level of service, the rates are not exorbitant. In addition, if one night's rent is paid in advance, your room will be reserved no matter how late you arrive.

Activities

Facilities on the property include a fifteen-station, mile-long course for joggers, two excellent hard-surfaced tennis courts, free to guests, and a nine-hole par three pitch and putt golf course. Hidden Valley public golf course is only a few minutes away in Cottage Grove.

Adjacent to the lodge is a heated swimming pool, with a nearby wading pool and playground for children. The Bowling Green, a bowl-

Station house of The Village Green Railroad

ing alley with twelve lanes, is right across the street.

In addition, a trip on The Village Green Railroad deserves special mention. The Goose, the hotel's private excursion steam-engine train, runs only in the summer, but when it does, the ride is an experience not to be missed. The station, located behind the tennis courts, is also a museum of old railroad lore and equipment. The excursion itself is a two-and-a-half hour trip back into the time when railroad logging was the backbone of Oregon's economy. The train steams along the Rogue River, through majestic forests, into the Calapoaga Mountains, and to the old Bohemia gold mine, its final destination. There it stops so that passengers can stretch their legs and inspect the abandoned mine buildings and shafts. It is a nostalgic trip for those who remember the locomotives of times past. And for younger visitors, it is an experience that otherwise may not be repeated, for there are very few of the old "lokys" left anywhere in the United States.

After the train ride and dinner in the hotel's Iron Maiden, look in on its piano bar in the Captain's Cabin—a relaxing cap to the evening.

Dining

A life-size statue known as the Iron Maiden greets guests at the entrance to the dining room, named in her honor. She has quite a history—including survival of the great Chicago fire—and legend has it she brings good fortune wherever she goes. Pleasant evenings and fine food being the rule here, maybe the legend is true.

Her namesake is an elegantly rustic room with a huge copper-hooded brick fireplace dominating one end. High-backed, upholstered booths and overstuffed chairs contribute both comfort and privacy. The menu measures up to the decor. Each day a particular dinner selection—usually exotic fare at a set price—is featured; the other items on the menu are equally interesting. The service is experienced and attentive, adding immeasurably to the enjoyment of the occasion. Prices range from medium to high. For dinner in the Iron Maiden, men should wear jackets, women dresses or evening pants suits.

The Village Green's coffee shop, the Copper Rooster, is open for breakfast, lunch, and dinner and offers early-American decor, excellent food, and quick service.

During the summer when the weather is good, it is often pleasant to have a meal at poolside where full luncheon and bar service is provided between 11:00 A.M. and 3:00 P.M.

Checklist

House
    House key
    Babysitter and dog-sitter
        arranged
    Doors and windows locked
    Furnace turned down
    Water and electric lights
        turned off
    Neighbor to take in mail and
        newspapers arranged

Packing
    Casual clothes
    Dinner clothes
    Walking shoes
    Bathing suits and robes
    Toilet articles

Personal
    Money and checkbook
    Glasses and sunglasses
    Reservation confirmations
    Camera and film

Sports Equipment
    Binoculars
    Bicycles
    Tennis gear
    Golf gear
    Fishing tackle
    Clamming equipment
    Rain gear
    Skiing gear
    Rucksack

Refreshments
    Thermos of coffee
    Breakfast ingredients
    Beverages
    Snacks

Auto
    Extra set of car keys
    Chains (in winter)
    Full gas tank

Other Books from Pacific Search Press

The Apple Cookbook by Kyle D. Fulwiler
Asparagus: The Sparrowgrass Cookbook by Autumn Stanley
The Bean Cookbook: Dry Legume Cookery by Norma S. Upson
The Berry Cookbook by Kyle D. Fulwiler
The Birdhouse Book: Building Houses, Feeders, and Baths
    by Don McNeil
Bone Appétit! Natural Food for Pets by Frances Sheridan Goulart
Border Boating: Twelve Cruises through the San Juan and Gulf Islands
    by Phyllis and Bill Bultmann
Butterflies Afield in the Pacific Northwest
    by William Neill/Douglas Hepburn, photography
Canning and Preserving without Sugar by Norma M. MacRae, R.D.
The Carrot Cookbook by Ann Saling
Cascade Companion by Susan Schwartz/Bob and Ira Spring, photography
The Chilkat Dancing Blanket by Cheryl Samuel
Common Seaweeds of the Pacific Coast by J. Robert Waaland
The Complete Guide to Organic Gardening West of the Cascades
    by Steve Solomon
The Crawfish Cookbook by Norma S. Upson
Cross-Country Downhill and Other Nordic Mountain Skiing Techniques
    (2d Ed. Revised & Enlarged) by Steve Barnett
Cruising the Columbia and Snake Rivers: Eleven Cruises in the
    Inland Waterway by Sharlene P. Nelson and Joan LeMieux
The Dogfish Cookbook by Russ Mohney
The Eggplant Cookbook by Norma S. Upson
Fire and Ice: The Cascade Volcanoes (Revised Ed.)
    by Stephen L. Harris
A Fish Feast by Charlotte Wright
Food 101: A Student Guide to Quick and
    Easy Cooking by Cathy Smith
The Getaway Guide II: More Short Vacations in the Pacific Northwest
    by Marni and Jake Rankin
The Getaway Guide III: Short Vacations in Northern California
    by Marni and Jake Rankin
The Getaway Guide IV: Short Vacations in Southern California
    by Marni and Jake Rankin
The Green Tomato Cookbook by Paula Simmons
The Guide to Successful Tapestry Weaving by Nancy Harvey
The Handspinner's Guide to Selling by Paula Simmons
The House Next Door: Seattle's Neighborhood Architecture
    by Lila Gault/Mary Randlett, photography
Little Mammals of the Pacific Northwest by Ellen B. Kritzman
Living Shores of the Pacific Northwest
    by Lynwood Smith/Bernard Nist, photography
Make It and Take It: Homemade Gear for Camp and Trail
    by Russ Mohney

Marine Mammals of Eastern North Pacific and Arctic Waters
      edited by Delphine Haley
Messages from the Shore by Victor B. Scheffer
Minnie Rose Lovgreen's Recipe for Raising Chickens
      by Minnie Rose Lovgreen
Mushrooms 'n Bean Sprouts: A First Step for Would-be Vegetarians
      by Norma M. MacRae, R.D.
My Secret Cookbook by Paula Simmons
The Natural Fast Food Cookbook by Gail L. Worstman
The Natural Fruit Cookbook by Gail L. Worstman
The Northwest Adventure Guide by Pacific Search Press
The Pike Place Market: People, Politics, and Produce
      by Alice Shorett and Murray Morgan
Rhubarb Renaissance: A Cookbook by Ann Saling
The River Pioneers: Early Days on Grays Harbor by Edwin Van Syckle
Roots & Tubers: A Vegetable Cookbook by Kyle D. Fulwiler
The Salmon Cookbook by Jerry Dennon
Seattle Photography by David Barnes
Sleek & Savage: North America's Weasel Family by Delphine Haley
Spinning and Weaving with Wool by Paula Simmons
Starchild & Holahan's Seafood Cookbook
      by Adam Starchild and James Holahan
They Tried to Cut It All by Edwin Van Syckle
Two Crows Came by Jonnie Dolan
Warm & Tasty: The Wood Heat Stove Cookbook by Margaret Byrd Adams
The White-Water River Book: A Guide to Techniques, Equipment,
      Camping, and Safety by Ron Watters/Robert Winslow, photography
The Whole Grain Bake Book by Gail L. Worstman
Wild Mushroom Recipes by Puget Sound Mycological Society
Wild Shrubs: Finding and Growing Your Own by Joy Spurr
The Zucchini Cookbook by Paula Simmons